STILL
STANDING

STILL STANDING

ACCIDENTAL LIFE LESSONS

A True Story of the Long Walk Back
from Traumatic Brain Injury

Major Steven R. Hirst, USAF, Ret.

BLASTER PUBLICATIONS / COLORADO SPRINGS, COLORADO

Blaster Publications
Colorado Springs, Colorado

ISBN 978-0-9855173-0-4

Editor and Creative Advisor: *Ann Ryan Solomon*
Cover design: *Range of Designs*
Page design and layout: *FerberDesign*

I would like to dedicate this book to the millions of other

people who suffer from Traumatic Brain Injury (TBI),

and to their families who stand by their sides.

CONTENTS

FOREWORD

This book is an inspiration to all: to those like myself who have lived charmed lives, and to those like my friend Steve who have suffered inconceivable misfortune. Steve Hirst is the type of person who cannot be ignored. His infectious personality exudes a positive nature combined with a driven work ethic. That is what brought him to my attention the first time I saw him on a basketball court. He obviously had a great deal of fun playing the game and it was evidenced by his frenetic hustle and pure joy for the competitive nature of the sport.

During my tenure as an assistant coach at the US Air Force Academy, I observed Steve on the junior varsity team as a cadet with no previous military experience; he was obviously much like me when I was a cadet—clueless!

It is quite a change for any easy-going, happy and relatively unconcerned young person to land in a culture like the Academy—totally foreign, isolated and downright intimi-

Coach Gregg Popovich and
Steve "Blaster" Hirst

dating. When the shock lifted and Steve realized it was time to compete, study, and figure it out, he was no longer adrift, but rather a master of his thoughts and aspirations.

Once I left USAFA to pursue a head coaching job, I lost contact with Steve and many years later learned of his tragic accident through another former player who I did coach at the varsity level, Tim Harris. It was horrifying to discover that this competitor and free spirit was now limited in so many agonizing ways.

We quickly reconnected and I began to meet Steve at our Spurs basketball games when we played in Denver. On these occasions I would actually prepare myself to show no pity, speak to him as I used to, with directness, humor, sarcasm and motivation, and try to show him we were all so proud of him in so many ways.

The frustration and anger he must feel—or perhaps I project how I would feel under similar circumstances—is palpable to me and I am awestruck to still see the Hirst smile fighting its way through the unresponsive and ungiving nature of traumatic brain injury. This unique spirit pervades his entire being and he is the same on the inside, though TBI fights him minute by minute.

What a warrior, even more than he ever was as an F-15 pilot! His strength, resolve and persistence are more than I can imagine. I only hope he can keep it up and, with the love and support he has received from friends and family (his wife is beyond description), I believe he will continue to improve.

The drastic shift from fit, unencumbered F-15 pilot to physical dependency in a matter of seconds is an unimaginable life changer and this story relates the honest, heartfelt mental and emotional processes that take place on such a journey. Horrifying as it was and is, Blaster shows that his spirit, personality and love of life cannot be snuffed out.

Go get 'em, Blaster!

Sincerely,

Gregg Popovich
President & Head Basketball Coach
San Antonio Spurs

PREFACE

Traumatic Brain Injury is defined as a blow or jolt to the head or a penetrating injury that disrupts brain function. Steve's TBI was severe, including an extended period of unconsciousness and amnesia. Even mild TBI injuries can cause headaches, nausea, dizziness, excessive fatigue, concentration and memory problems, irritability, and disturbances in balance, vision, and sleep. In the military, the Defense and Veterans Brain Injury Center (DVBIC) identifies the leading causes of TBI as bullets, fragments, and blasts; falls; motor vehicle and traffic crashes; and assaults.

The Centers for Disease Control and Prevention (CDC) estimates that 1.7 million people sustain a traumatic brain injury each year, resulting in 1.4 million emergency department visits, 275,000 hospitalizations and 52,000 deaths. TBI is a contributing factor to a third of all injury-related deaths in the United States.

Before Steve's injury in 1996, most research related to TBI was related to head injuries in civilian populations, such as car accidents and falls. The University of Virginia started to use the Sports as a Laboratory Assessment Model, or SLAM, to study concussion and mild traumatic brain injury in college football players. The tragic increase of TBI in military personnel has brought it into the national spotlight, along with new discoveries about the effects of TBI and concussion on professional athletes, youth in sports, and geriatric populations.

Military personnel in both combat and noncombat situations are at high risk for TBI. A 2008 study by the RAND Corporation found that one in five service members returning from Iraq or Afghanistan have screened positive for TBI. In 2000, the direct and indirect costs of TBI in the military totaled an estimated $60 billion. But DVBIC also observes that, despite recent attention to combat-related TBI, the injury "is not uncommon even in garrison and occurs during usual daily activities," such as physical training and leisure pursuits.

The Veterans Administration has made TBI a major focus, especially as it relates to veterans returning to civilian life, requiring health care and vocational retraining. Ironically, the largest increase in TBI for veterans is not younger returning soldiers, but the aging population, as they enter into their 70s and 80s, due to injuries from falls, sometimes resulting in high levels of disability.

The DVBIC looked to the earlier research on sports concussion when assessing and planning for the dramatic increase in military cases of TBI. DVBIC brought military and civilian head injury and sports medicine experts together to discuss the similarities between combat blast injuries and sports concussions. Together they developed *Clinical*

Practice Guidelines for the Assessment and Management of Concussion and TBI.

Blast injuries are more common, more complex, and often more severe than sports concussions. But, according to Jeffrey T. Barth, PhD, of the University of Virginia School of Medicine and DVBIC–Charlottesville Rehabilitation Programs, the lessons learned from sports medicine have guided better understanding and awareness of combat TBI, and its assessment and management.

In *The Concussion Crisis: Anatomy of a Silent Epidemic* (Carroll and Rosner, 2011), TBI is described as "the signature wound" of the Iraq and Afghanistan wars. TBI and Post Traumatic Stress Disorder, commonly known as PTSD, are often concurrent and related. The anger and rage so often associated with PTSD is more common in soldiers who have sustained a TBI. The book quotes the descriptions of many top specialists in TBI. James Hill, MD, a neurologist at Yale University, said TBI "is like dropping a computer," and Warren Lux, MD, a neurologist and former acting director of DVBIC, observed that "brain injuries, like amputations, are for life."

Awareness of TBI has increased dramatically since Steve's accident in 1996. But there is still much to be done in the research and treatment of this condition, which has quietly and suddenly become an epidemic and major public health issue. One of Steve's primary goals in writing his book is to bring awareness and support to TBI victims and those who care for them.

Col. Bob Ireland, USAF, Medical Corps, Chief Flight Surgeon, (Ret.), served more than twenty-four years in the Air Force. During Steve's last year at Kadena Air Base in Okinawa (1989–1990), Ireland was the squadron's flight surgeon. He later specialized in neuropsychiatry and went on to serve in leadership positions for Air Force aerospace medicine and at the Pentagon as the Program Director for Mental Health Policy.

"Our nation is beginning to see that we are unprepared to deal with the number and severity of head injuries incurred by service members over the past decades," says Dr. Ireland. "Those who incur significant brain injuries cannot simply be 'patched up,' and sent home to continue their lives with their families. Enormous resources will be required for meaningful and sustained support for those with traumatic brain injuries, and for their families who are also injured in a significant way."

One of the leading experts on TBI, PTSD and suicide in the military, Dr. Ireland served as spokesperson on these issues for the United States Department of Defense before his retirement. He has contributed background notes specific to Steve's story, and to TBI in general, throughout this book. Dr. Ireland's notes are designated with a small brain icon.

HIGH FLIGHT

By John Gillespie Magee, Jr.

Oh! I have slipped the surly bonds of earth

And danced the skies on laughter-silvered wings;

Sunward I've climbed, and joined the tumbling mirth

Of sun-split clouds, and done a hundred things

You have not dreamed of, wheeled and soared and swung

High in the sunlit silence. Hov'ring there,

I've chased the shouting wind along, and flung

My eager craft through footless halls of air.

Up, up the long, delirious, burning blue

I've topped the wind-swept heights with easy grace

Where never lark, or even eagle flew,

And, while with silent lifting mind I've trod

The high untrespassed sanctity of space,

Put out my hand and touched the face of God.

Major Stephen R. Hirst, September 27, 1994.

INTRODUCTION

A VERY BUMPY LANDING

I am an author completely by accident. No kidding.

I never would have thought to write a book about my life if that life had followed its scheduled flight plan. But I traded the controls of a fighter jet for the less precise engineering of a wheelchair. I went from the perfect lay-up of my favorite sport to the humbling floor burn of the bathroom fall, and the occasional dribble with no ball in sight.

I used to hold the love of my life in my arms as we doted on our baby daughters, proud of our shared education at the United States Air Force Academy, secure in the promise that we would serve and retire, maybe run a little bratwurst stand somewhere, someday.

My story was going to be about a random stretch of black ice on a cold Alaskan road one beautiful afternoon. I probably should have lost my life that day, but it turns out I'm still here.

I'm still a husband, a father, a son, a brother, a colleague and a friend. I've had to learn and re-learn how to walk and talk and take care of myself, instead of being independent and taking care of others. I've learned how to ask for help, sometimes scream for it. I've learned to depend on other people and even a beloved canine companion.

From the sports star to the guy in the chair, I've been ripped off, almost run over in a retail parking lot, ignored, pitied, stared at and ridiculed. I'm still recovering and I'm not stopping. I've been working on this a long time now, and so the story has evolved beyond just me and my accident. It's about the lessons I never would have learned, despite my previous and privileged education, my perfect life, my very acceptable free throw, my service record and my certain future. Thinking I had lost all that is part of the story, but there is more to it. And it keeps getting more interesting.

I've learned the woman I love has been the strongest wind beneath my wings, not the lift of an F-15 take-off. I love her with a love that can only be forged from the depths of despair, depression, understanding and loyalty. We watch our daughters, now young and successful women, and we marvel.

I've learned what love really means, from my wife and daughters and my mother, my family and friends, and from a service dog. Finally, I've learned from understanding myself a bit more than fighter pilots normally allow themselves. The people that know me know that I am still here. The people that do not know me have taught me many lessons, some inspiring, others embarrassing and ignorant.

So, my story has taught me things I never knew I would have to learn, things to share about understanding and accepting. There is no way I would have learned these lessons myself, if not by accident. My brain is still here with me, for better or for traumatic brain injury. There are so many young soldiers coming back from Iraq and Afghanistan with traumatic brain injuries, and many others that land in this strange world for different reasons. Please think of them and help as you read about my experience.

With a traumatic brain injury, I have had some memory loss. What I do remember, I have written. I have also relied on friends, family, public, and medical records and other resources to add perspective through background notes in each chapter.

There may be a few rough words, and I'm not going to hold back and pretend this has been a fairy tale. I come from, and married into, people who do not complain, yet it has been harder for them than it has for me. I should also warn readers that the unofficial language of Wisconsin, sarcasm, is used heavily.

But as you read this, please know how grateful I am for all the love and support that surrounds me, allowing me to tell you more than just my bad-luck tale. It's really more about the big lessons in life, some more accidental than others.

Still Standing,

Major Steven R. Hirst, USAF, Ret.

STILL STANDING

January 13, 1996. Anchorage, Alaska.

PART ONE

GROUNDED DREAMS

Okinawa, Japan, circa 1989.

CHAPTER ONE

BLASTER TO BLACK ICE

The thirteenth of January 1996, was a beautiful day in Anchorage, Alaska, chilly with clear skies. At least that's what people tell me. I really have no idea. I can't remember, even though it was the day that changed my life.

I had recently arrived at Elmendorf Air Force Base in Alaska to fly the F-15 Eagle fighter jet for the United States Air Force as part of the 54th Fighter Squadron, "The Leopards." Every pilot has a handle, usually bestowed by the other pilots. Mine was Blaster, earned during my days at Kadena Air Base in Okinawa, Japan. More about that later, but let's just say I didn't let anything around the plane get in my way when I was ready to go.

I was an Air Force F-15 pilot when there were not many F-15 pilots in the United States, or in the world. I try to be modest, but truthfully, we were the best. The F-15s would sit alert in other countries, but only United States pilots, maintenance people and intelligence folks ever got to see these fighter jets up close.

There was no better air superiority fighter in the world at the time. They are beautiful machines. There are newer fighter planes operational now, but among pilots who flew the Eagle, we still agree it's the best. Nothing will change my opinion.

I was thirty-six years old. I was fit, healthy, and happy with my career and my personal life. I had no worries. I was on top of the world when I was flying the F-15. I felt invincible.

My wife, Susan, and our two daughters, Stephanie and Stacey, were in Alabama, where Susan was on assignment for her own duties in the Air Force. The holidays were over and I was back at work. The second week of January had been a good one, and I had flown several times.

Saturday was my day off, so I worked out at the base gym. Lifting weights and stretching is always a huge part of a pilot's schedule, flying or nonflying. I played intramural basketball to stay in shape, and I was playing on three different Air Force teams, part of my ongoing affair with the sport. But basketball only lasted a few months, so I had always worked out by lifting weights and doing aerobic exercise on the stationary bike, treadmill and running outside to stay in shape for flying. The ability to withstand nine Gs of force, nine times the force of gravity once flying again, is why a pilot in a nonflying job would continue to work out just the same as a pilot with a flying job.

I was nearing my nonflying days. My next assignment after Elmendorf was probably going to be a staff job, similar to the one I had just held at Langley Air Force Base before coming to Alaska. Or, if I were lucky, I might have gone on to command a squadron somewhere, just to stay flying another two years. The emphasis was on performing as well as one could in the current job, so I didn't dwell too much on what might come next.

I had rented an apartment off-base, and the fridge was empty. After my workout at the base gym, I did my first grocery shopping at the Commissary, the military grocery store on almost any US military base in the world. The roads were icy, but I was a safe driver. Being from Wisconsin, I had plenty of experience driving on snow and ice.

After picking up a few groceries, I headed home. It was about 1:45 in the afternoon. The receipt in my pocket indicated I had great intentions for a clean and healthy lifestyle. I had chosen an array of cleaning products and produce, including Brussels sprouts.

I was on DeBarr Road curve, between Lake Otis Parkway and Airport Heights Road. Driving at just under thirty-five miles per hour, the posted speed limit, I suddenly hit a patch of black ice. The police later confirmed my speed. I lost control, the car spun out on the ice and wrapped around a light pole. When it hit the pole, the car came to a dead stop, but things inside my head kept moving. My brain was scrambled as it met my skull.

The pole crushed through the driver's door and violently whipped my head. The car was stopped, but my brain continued moving forward and bounced around inside. It only took a few seconds, and everything I know about what happened comes from what other people tell me, even the fact that it was such a nice day. I have no memory of it. Nothing at all. Sometimes I think it would be better to have some memories, even though I'm thankful I don't remember the pain.

But it isn't only that day and the days that followed that I do not remember. Many of the things that happened before the accident are no longer in my brain. Not having those memories is very humiliating and hard to accept. For example, I don't remember my father dying. He died on June 23, 1993 at the age of sixty-seven, over two years before my accident. That is something I wish I could remember.

I don't even remember flying by the stadium during a Florida vs. Florida State football game in 1995. I was going through F-15 retraining at Tyndall AFB in Florida before going to Alaska. The squadron was tasked to support the flyover, to usher in the National Anthem before the game. I was honored to fly in the formation. The event went well, I'm told. The noise and spectacle of flyovers were always a hit with the stadium crowds, and few were louder than a four-ship of F-15s. You could feel the sound. We were recognized at halftime—my wife Susan tells me about all of it. I'm sure it was one of the proudest moments in my life. I'm sure it was like walking on water in the stadium. But I don't remember it.

It didn't take long for the accident to happen, maybe a few seconds from the time I started to spin until I hit the light pole, but the concept of time for me has changed forever. I do remember before the car accident I was a pretty good athlete, and I was a damn good F-15 pilot.

All the years I spent in a plane flying dangerous missions were overtaken by an everyday drive coming home from the store. Never again would I fly the greatest fighter jet ever built for the United States Air Force. Never again would I look at life or people in the same ways. Blaster had hit black ice.

OTHER PERSPECTIVES

Susan Hirst, *Wife*

I'll never forget the phone call which brought to reality a change in our lives that had taken place hours before. Steve was in Alaska for a dream assignment, flying the plane he loved. I was in Alabama attending Air Command and Staff College—something I was very happy about. Our daughters Stephanie and Stacey were with me, because for ten months I would be in one place and have a lot of time at home. My mother-in-law, Mag, was in town taking care of the girls with me. I had been to Toronto for a four-day exchange with the Canadian Defense Force. Shortly after I returned home, we went out for a quick Chinese meal. Our girls wanted to play flashlight tag, so, we needed to get home before the night had passed. Once we were home I went to call Steve at his apartment. I hadn't talked to him for several days while I'd been in Canada, but he'd been on the phone all but one night with his mom and our daughters. He had moved into his apartment on Friday and I figured I'd be his first phone call. As I reached for the phone I noticed the message light blinking—our lives were forever altered.

Steve Ulik, *High School Friend*

My ex-wife, Rose, was from Alaska, and had moved back home after we divorced. She opened up the *Anchorage Times* on January 14 and saw a horrible photo of a serious car accident, right above the obituaries for the day. When she read the caption, she called me immediately. It was Hirsty in the car.

Chris Riordan, *Neighborhood and High School Friend*

I got a call in the middle of the night. Our friend Steve Ulik's ex-wife Rose had read about Steve's accident in the newspaper and called very worried. He was in the hospital, it was very serious and he had a head injury. He was all alone up there. We didn't know what to expect. We just hoped he wouldn't die.

What remained of my car.

CHAPTER TWO

BRAIN CRASH

It took the rescue crew about forty-five minutes to get me out of the car and then to the hospital. I look at the photo that was taken at the accident scene, and I wonder how I survived. I don't remember a thing about it.

At Alaska's Our Lady of Providence Medical Center, I was stabilized and assessed. I did not have a lot of external injuries, but I was comatose with a closed head injury and I was in the ICU for four weeks. Then I was transferred to the VA hospital in Minneapolis. They had a team of experts in neurological trauma and I was air-transported on February 10. Meanwhile, my family and friends were mobilizing and were at my side when I arrived, not that I was aware of their presence.

The first thing I can remember was waking up at the Minneapolis Veterans Hospital, after I had been there a while. I had never felt physically like this before. The left side of my body was unusable. I couldn't talk. I couldn't eat. I couldn't sleep. I wondered, and continued to wonder, "What the hell happened to me?!" I wanted to know from The Man Upstairs: "Why was I chosen to go through this?!" I still want to know.

I don't remember waking up or coming out of my coma. I don't remember what my feelings were, but they must not have been very good, because my mother, my wife, and my children have never said anything nice about my reactions. I was angry and frustrated and could barely communicate.

I saw my wife Susan a lot, but I guess I don't remember just how much she was there with me.

Our daughters were still in Alabama attending grade school, but Susan continued to travel to Minneapolis as often as she could, while others watched the girls. I would upset her constantly by wanting to know why she never came to visit me. And how was the guy she was seeing?! Nice, huh?! As if she would have had any time to even look at another guy, while working, taking care of our daughters and flying back and forth to deal with me.

My mother, Mag, moved to Minneapolis from Milwaukee, and rented a small furnished apartment nearby. She was with me every day at the hospital, then Susan would come up during the weekends, to give her a break.

The word had spread and, apparently, I had many visitors while I was in and out of the coma. I do remember one friend coming to see me in Minneapolis. Dick Stadler came to see me and my family. But I can't remember any of my pilot friends visiting, though many did, including Bobby Renaud, Fester, Gonzo, and their wives. Childhood friends Chris Riordan, Steve Ulik, Chris and Loni Hagerup, and my teacher and coach Jack Bleier also came to visit. Other than family, I cannot remember anybody else coming to see me. My memory has done some weird things.

I saw our children on occasion. I really missed our daughters, watching them play sports and seeing them improve in school. They were quite upset at what had happened to me, and they couldn't get me to react the way I did before as their Dad. This eventually turned into resentment at the way my personality was changed. I was impolite and vulgar.

Much later, Susan told me I said some bad things to her and to my mother. The names I called them and the things I said to them were inexcusable. I had no right saying those things, yet now I know this is very common in people who have traumatic brain injuries.

I didn't remember the crash, or calling people names. Some of my memories of things that happened before the accident completely disappeared, and the first few months after the crash I remember little to nothing. It's funny how that works being in a deep coma, as I was for a full month. The doctors think I was in a partial coma for a time after that.

I do remember how depressed I was. My family thought I was still in a coma for a while, but I may have been so depressed I could barely respond. I don't remember much, but I can remember the heaviness and the fog, just feeling numb.

I had never thought about having constant depression and anger. Before the accident, I remember being angry or sad sometimes, but nothing like this. I would hear people around me talk about me still being in a coma and I couldn't respond. It gave new meaning to the word despondent—you literally cannot react. Whenever I was even slightly depressed or down in the dumps, their talk made me very detached, and I would mentally disappear. I was scared of being angry, so I'd just mentally check out. This went on for a long, long time.

I think I began coming out of the depression when I started recognizing and listening to people who came to visit me. Being so close to my hometown in Wisconsin made it easier for the many friends who visited me at the VA hospital.

Things entered a different phase when I finally realized I still had a life to live, which included two daughters and a wife, and I had to make sure they lived their lives to the fullest. I made a conscious choice to pull myself back from darker thoughts and self-pity.

Now it was time to make a plan. My external physical injuries had healed. There was a lot to consider as we learned what it was going to take to live with TBI. The doctors told me I would need therapy: physical therapy, occupational therapy, speech therapy and psychological counseling. We had a lot to think about. I had no idea how much I was about to learn.

OTHER PERSPECTIVES

Susan Hirst, *Wife*

Steve looked good with the exception of tubes and wraps and monitor. I don't know what I expected, but he looked pretty good. No obvious bruises or cuts, just a sleeping man with a pressure monitor protruding from his skull and a breathing tube rammed down his throat. For the next four weeks our lives were suspended in time and place. We lived from 7 a.m. to 7 p.m. in the ICU. Nothing has been the same since.

Chris Riordan, *Neighborhood and High School Friend*

Ulik and I drove up to Minneapolis together, not sure what to expect. As we were going into Steve's hospital room, our high school math teacher and basketball coach, Jack Bleier was walking out. Our friends Chris and Loni Hagerup had also traveled up. It was intense.

Steve had a lot of tubes coming out of him, and he couldn't talk. His eyes would follow certain people and it was clear he had some recognition of certain individuals. Beyond that, it was hard to tell.

Jack Bleier, *High School Coach and Teacher*

When I heard that Steve had been involved in a car accident in Alaska, the word was that the car he was driving slipped on a patch of black ice and ended up running into a pole. In the accident, his brain had been "shaken," and he was in a coma with his future uncertain. We learned that he was moved to a VA hospital in Minneapolis. By this time I think that his mom, Mag, had gone there to be with him. My wife and I were among those that made a trip to Minneapolis to see Steve, but my recollections of the trip are not that vivid. I believe Steve was still in a coma at the time. I think it was Mag who then told us about the unreal ordeal that Steve's wife, Susan, was going through. She was also an officer in the Air Force and was stationed in Alabama at the time. She had duties on base Monday thru Friday, was raising their two little girls, and then flying up to Minneapolis EVERY weekend to be with Steve—even though he was in a coma a good part of that time. From everything I have heard, Susan has devotedly been by Steve's side through every day of this extremely difficult experience. Talk about sainthood. And as time moved on, people have kept me in touch with just how much stress this accident has put on his family, especially Susan and their two girls. Talk about a profile in courage.

A MEDICAL PERSPECTIVE

Dr. Bob Ireland, *Surgeon Specialist and Friend*

Commonly in motor vehicle accidents, traumatic brain injuries involve critical structures and pathways in the front (anterior) part of the brain called the prefrontal cortex. Unlike areas of the brain involved in movement and bodily sensations, the higher (dorsal) prefrontal cortex and its connections mediate executive functions that include paying attention, processing information, planning and initiating actions, and importantly, inhibiting reflexive actions. The lower (ventral) prefrontal cortex is involved with emotions. After prefrontal cortical trauma it is not uncommon for inappropriate behaviors to occur due to poor prefrontal functioning, resulting in what can be grossly inappropriate disinhibited behaviors. Brain trauma may also affect one's ability to encode, store, and retrieve memories. This can result in confabulation, the unintentional expression of false memories and sometimes attempting to act upon them.

Thus, the results of traumatic brain injuries can be devastating, as one can become completely disinhibited while acting upon distorted and false memories. Families and friends struggle to understand the behaviors as results of the injuries, but cannot help but experience intense emotional pain and conflict in response to inappropriate remarks and behaviors. Sustaining hope for healing can be very difficult as neurological improvement after trauma usually emerges slowly and may not fully resolve, or in some cases improve at all. It is normal to wonder if a loved one is still "there" or will ever return. This produces a profound mixture of reactive anger and grief mixed with hope, challenging the executive functioning of families, friends, and medical staff themselves who are trying to inhibit their own emotional reactions (including anger) to outrageous behaviors.

CHAPTER THREE

TRAUMATIC BRAIN INJURY IS TRAUMATIC

The doctors call what I suffered from my car accident, Traumatic Brain Injury, or TBI. The clinical words don't come even close to capturing the total life-changing unfairness of it all. Unfortunately, I'm not sure I can truly describe TBI to anybody who hasn't gone through it, except to try and share my own experience.

Externally, I had only minor cuts and a few bruises from the accident. But my brain was seriously damaged. My brain didn't stop moving until after the car did, bouncing against my skull. People said I looked a little different, not too bad. But, of course, they couldn't see my brain.

Much later after my hospital stay, Susan told me I said some bad things to her and to my mother. The names I called them and the things I said to them were absolutely rotten. I don't remember any of that, but since then, I have had a lot of experience with anger and depression, learning how to control one and manage the other.

Years later, I still have a terrible memory, but in some ways it's getting better. Sometimes I think something has been wiped out of my brain forever, and then it mysteriously returns. I can honestly say I've progressed more since leaving inpatient therapy, but it's like going to school and then doing your homework. It's hard work.

I do remember what the many therapists taught me about talking, walking, or cooking a meal. Since I was in a partial coma for a long time, the doctors told me I might never remember what I'd been like. But the memory loss is so random. I do remember growing up, going to all my schools, getting married to the world's greatest woman, and flying the world's greatest fighter jet. I didn't want to accept that my memory was completely gone. Once I could get back on a computer, I started writing my story.

There are no sure answers for anyone who has experienced a very serious car accident with a TBI. Since January 13th, 1996, my life has been nothing short of a struggle to make anything happen the way it should. This injury has profoundly altered my life.

But I'm not the only one battling TBI. I didn't have spinal cord damage like Christopher Reeve. I didn't lose an arm or a leg, like so many soldiers coming back with TBIs after their service. I try to appreciate how far I have come, but I wish TBI could get the research, attention and action it deserves for the thousands of veterans, athletes and everyday people unlucky enough to meet up with this frustrating challenge.

The way some people look at me and speak to me, because of my TBI, can make me feel very self-conscious and stupid. But I know I was not a stupid person before I was hurt. When people at a large grocery or department store don't really understand me, I wish they would just slow down their thinking and it might come to them. I'm better understood than I used to be, so things are improving.

And it goes both ways. When I have a lot on my mind, I try to get it out too fast and things get lost between my thoughts and my words. If they fail to understand me the first time, I try to slow down my speaking and change the words to give people something they can understand. Sometimes it works, sometimes it doesn't. And most of the time it is my fault, but I'm getting better at speaking all the time.

Precrash, if I was taking a shower and the TV was on, I would have only been interested in sports. Now, the only thing I'm interested in is weather, because I get cold so easily. I used to get a little interested in the weather when I was flying, but when you're flying an all-weather jet like the Eagle, you could care less about the weather because you can fly over it.

It's the things I used to take for granted that can be so heartbreaking. I couldn't drive anymore, so my wife had to drive our family everywhere. I couldn't help drive the kids to all their activities or teach them how to drive like my dad taught me. But, on the flip side, I have become an expert in the use of public transportation and I have a type rating in motorized wheelchair transportation.

TBI is a very tough thing. Some friends treat you rather weirdly afterward. I don't think it is because they don't care. Maybe it's just too much for them to handle. Those who do not live with this injury, do not understand what it is like. Period. Dot. They cannot understand what it is like to be a spouse of someone with a TBI. They do not understand what it is like to feel like a burden, or to feel so burdened.

I hate hearing and I'm sure I will hate hearing, certain things for the remainder of my life. "Can't you stop doing that?! I've never seen you do that before!" It happens all the time at the dinner table post-TBI when I choke on food, spill things or drink the wrong way. Imagine, a fighter pilot being told he is drinking the wrong way!

I work hard every day on not choking or spilling everywhere, but it's not always something I can control. I think people feel there is no excuse for choking or spilling, but they forget that reflexes like swallowing are controlled by the brain. Your brain controls everything. I wonder how they would feel if they had a bad TBI for only a week.

If only there was an operation which would stop choking and spilling. And another operation to take the shaking out of my right shoulder and my left leg. Or a magic cure for arthritis—even people without TBIs would get behind that one.

If there were anything to alleviate or eliminate the effects of a TBI, I'd support it 100 percent. Because I'm not really OK, and I want to keep getting better.

OTHER PERSPECTIVES

Susan Hirst, *Wife*

Stephanie cried with me, Stacey was stoic. Each day, morning and night, at our Lady of Providence Hospital in Anchorage Alaska the girls greeted Steve and bid him good night. During the day they were entertained by Steve's squadron-mate families. They hadn't met us until that fateful time, but it didn't matter. We were embraced and cared for as dear family members.

Stephanie would come to Steve's side, hold his hand and share everything she had in her ten-year-old self. If he could hear, he experienced adventures of skating on glaciers, seeing moose wander freely, and meeting new friends at a new school. Stacey on the other hand did her duty. She said good morning and good night. She told her daddy she loved him. Nine years old by just a couple of weeks, Stacey said she'd talk to him later when he woke. This was the beginning of a new world for all of us.

For nearly five weeks Steve slept in the ICU. It wasn't peaceful and we didn't know what the future held. I had the unreal expectation that we would need a vacation later in the summer when this all ended. Little did I know that this would never end.

The next several months, until August, were spent with Steve in Minneapolis doing inpatient rehab at the VA Hospital. Steve's mom lived in a furnished apartment nearby, and spent Monday through Friday by his side. I went to school in Alabama each week and came back to Minneapolis each weekend. Stephanie and Stacey had their Grandpa, my dad, for a month and then spent each weekend with "strangers" from my school. I really don't know how we did it but on Fridays the girls would head out for the weekend in another home with another willing and supportive family while I'd make the flight to Minneapolis. The routine was somehow comforting but it wasn't until the girls visited Steve during their Spring Break that we knew he was there. For the first time, Steve "recognized" people he clearly knew and loved, his girls!

A MEDICAL PERSPECTIVE

Dr. Bob Ireland, *Surgeon Specialist and Friend*

The brain's moving after the car stopped (or in this case after the utility pole crushed the car's roof) refers to the phenomena of brain injury occurring in two places—where the external impact initially occurred ("coup") and on the opposite side of the brain where the moving brain "bounced" from the impact side ("countercoup"). The physics of this injury are thought to be enhanced by the compression of cerebral spinal fluid (which surrounds and normally protects the brain) into the area opposite the initial trauma, hydraulically driving the brain in the opposite direction, enhancing the second (countercoup) injury. Coup-countercoup injuries result in bruises (contusions) to the brain and can disrupt both neurons and supporting brain glial cells and their functions. This is usually associated with brain swelling which can be lethal if not surgically relieved.

This astonishing and articulate narrative about memory evokes ultimate questions about the nature of human existence and what it means to be a person. One is left wondering on what basis do pre-injury memories emerge? Are they arbitrary bursts of randomly improving neuronal functions that rise to consciousness, or an imaginative synthesis based upon more recent experiences? Countering the repugnant possibility that his current existence is based only upon learning about his prior life from others since his injury, Steve asserts what he confidently and increasingly remembers about life prior to the accident in spite of these memories seeming discontinuous and "so random." Based upon cellular-level biological theories related to post traumatic stress disorder research, one might speculate that memories with greater emotional valence (as opposed to simple declarative facts) are more retrievable. Thus, when considering Steve's account of what he does remember from the past, school experiences, marriage, and "flying the world's greatest fighter jet" emerge. One might speculate other early memories will continue to arise, likely most with higher levels of emotional valence.

On a philosophical level, it would be a mind-body dualistic error to tie Steve's identity as a person to one side or the other of the fence of the 1996 accident. A non-dualistic process philosophical perspective conceives of life, as a person, as a series of occasions of experience. In this way Steve is both who he was before and who he is now, as opposed to awaiting to be how he once was in the past. Steve's continuous and astonishing transformations in the face of lethal threats constitute his existence today.

In most ways, this journey is more challenging than the immensely challenging role of a F-15 jockey. Given the ThreatCon, Steve is blasting a way forward not imaginable after his initial injuries. More importantly, he does so now with humility and thankfulness, as he acknowledges regarding others with injuries, his could have been worse.

Anger likely had multiple dimensions making control an exhaustive challenge. From a biological perspective, rage can be unbridled due to impaired prefrontal cortical function and subsequent disinhibition per earlier discussion. Depressed mood is also associated with left frontal dysfunction. Even with recovery of prefrontal cortical function, reactive rage at suffering so many losses is an understandable outcome, especially for one whose performance capacity had exceeded that of ordinary mortals in several domains (a typical F-15 driver competitive perspective). From a psychodynamic perspective, many who suffer symptoms of major depression can be characterized as experiencing anger and rage directed inwardly against oneself. More understandably in this case, there is unspeakable grief over so many losses. After years of processing complicated changes, Steve transcends these challenges in his artful articulation of his struggle controlling anger and managing depression.

An early photo from St. Monica's Catholic Grade School.

PART TWO

EARLY LESSONS

My brother Dave (holding baby Tom), me, and Mike.

CHAPTER FOUR

THE GOLDEN YEARS

I was a pretty shy kid. I could blush like a beet if a teacher called on me. My quiet nature matched the quiet village where I grew up. I remember a general sense of happiness being raised in Whitefish Bay, Wisconsin, a suburb of Milwaukee. Known for its excellent schools and picture-perfect location on the shores of Lake Michigan, it was, and still is, an idyllic place for people to raise families. Many of my childhood friends have either stayed, or returned to raise their families or coach our teams—it has that kind of pull.

My father, John, "Jack" Hirst, was a counselor at three of the local grade schools, a job that hardly guaranteed fame or fortune, but certainly respect. He was also a coach. So, he knew a good thing in life when he saw it. But the original good thing he recognized early on was my mother, Mag, a few years behind him at their high school in Galena, Illinois, where they first met. Eventually they moved to The Bay to raise their family of six children in a place where their values of faith, family, hard work, and active recreation provided what I treasure as an ideal childhood.

My parents both grew up in Galena, Illinois. When we were growing up we often visited Galena, where my maternal grandfather worked at the Ulysses S. Grant historic home. My Grandfather Hirst was the Galena Postmaster and Chief of the Galena Volunteer Fire Department. My mother remembers the volunteer firefighting as the love of his life professionally. My father was an only child so we were the only grandchildren on that side. We kids always enjoyed, and my parents endured, the three-to-four-hour drive to see them, and our many other relatives.

I was the third of the six children. My eldest brother, Dave, was born in 1949, and the youngest, Dan, eighteen years later in 1967. Dave and my only sister, Sue, were like a second set of parents. They were nine and ten by the time I arrived on May 15, 1959, and not only helped take care of me, but were my earliest role models.

Dave, my eldest brother, is one of the hardest-working people I've ever known, an example that has influenced me for life. Sue, as the only daughter, with all those energetic brothers, was always a kind and loving influence, and has remained so, not

Me, with Dan, Tom, and Mike.

just for me, but for her children and all of us.

When Dave and Sue left home to pursue their adult lives, I was nine years old. I missed them greatly, to say the least—not that I ever said much. I was shy. Suddenly, I found myself in the unfamiliar role of eldest child to my three younger brothers, Mike, Tom and Dan. The ball was in my court.

My quiet nature and studious approach to both school and sports draped the mantle of miniature adult on my skinny shoulders, but I don't remember it ever being a burden. I was proud to be responsible and considered myself quite grown up.

The Village of Whitefish Bay is small, about a mile and a half long, north of Milwaukee along the western shore of Lake Michigan. For most of its 13,508 residents, and perhaps anyone lucky enough to have ever lived there, Whitefish Bay is a beautiful and magical spot. My large Catholic family was surrounded by other large Catholic families. It wasn't unusual for each of the families to have at least five children, giving all of us plenty of playmates. I met Chris Riordan in the second grade at St. Monica's. We were in Sister Savina's class, and we were pretty intimidated and both shy. Over the years we would hang out with small groups of other students and today we are still friends. We would cut through the Capper family's backyard to get to each other's houses, and Chris was like another son to my folks.

The neighborhood was full of kids, and we were always in someone's backyard or out in the street playing any sport we could think of. Frequently it was my father that organized events, including bringing home the hurdles from the high school and setting them up in the street so that we could have practice track meets in front of our house. The Capper family lived on the other side of our next-door neighbors and we wore a path through the backyards to get to each other. Greg Capper was the oldest in his family of nine kids, in between my age and my older siblings, and there was a Capper boy that matched up age-wise to all of us. Greg was the oldest of our group and a role model in sports and how to treat others.

My parents and the Cappers were also good friends, so it gave the neighborhood the feel of a very large extended family. We all played basketball in the Capper's backyard, which was mostly a concrete half-court, and we ran around like a sweaty band of sports nuts. My parents had a concrete slab for a garage in the yard when we moved to our Kent Avenue home when I was a year old. They had plans to build the garage, but put up a basketball hoop instead, and we enjoyed that far more than any garage. They finally built the garage when all the boys moved out.

In the summers we went to our family's two-bedroom cottage on Presque Isle Lake in the woods of northern Wisconsin. There were just two bedrooms, only cold

Mike, me, Tom, Sue, Dan, and Dave. Summer, 1981.

running water and no shower. There were always many children, some not Hirsts, but all were willingly adopted—it was wonderful.

We were there every weekend we could get away, plus a glorious two full weeks in August. Our friends were always welcome, so we were a busy base camp of happy kids. We explored and fished, water-skied, swam, trapped crabs and competed in everything. Mike was an amazing water-skier and Dave the consummate fisherman. Nothing pushes one's competitive buttons like brothers that are better than you at something. Or at everything!

Here is something I experienced, but do not remember. My mother was widowed June 23, 1993, when my father died from diabetes. I wish I could remember that, how he left us too soon. My mother Mag is a strong woman and learned how to cope very well. She had no idea what I had in store for her.

She now lives in Mequon, Wisconsin, near two of my brothers and sister Sue. My other brothers are living in Austin, Minnesota and Warwick, Rhode Island. All are amazing siblings to me and successful in their lives. I may not remember everything, but I remember how very much I loved my dad and my family then, and always. There are some things even a traumatic brain injury cannot erase.

When her six children were growing up my mom treated us all very well. When you are a little kid, or even a teen, I think it's safe to say you take your parents and the role models in your life a bit for granted. It will remain impossible for me to find the words, or for her to accept them, that describe exactly how wonderful my mom has always been. Not just to me, but to everyone.

We lived in a nice town, but we didn't have very much money. She sacrificed on things she may have wanted or needed so she could buy things for us. She is a true believer in God, and her faith has always been with her. When I asked her once, "Why did God allow my brain injury?" I didn't know I would need three hours to spare for the answer! Of course it's a loaded question, but she can go on for hours if I'm foolish enough to ask it.

She has been there with me, along with the rest of my family through everything. She is strong and sensible, attributes I recognized early when I met my wife Susan. I look back on those golden years with gratitude and happiness—I really believe I had the storybook childhood.

OTHER PERSPECTIVES

Mag Hirst, *Mother*

Steve was never a troublemaker. He loved to play outside with the many other children in the neighborhood. We lived on a block with about a hundred kids and they would all get together to play year-round. They would skate in somebody's backyard where a sprinkler could freeze an ice rink in the winter, and they would jump into piles of leaves in the fall. It really was a great place for kids.

Chris Riordan, *Neighborhood and High School Friend*

I just about lived at the Hirst's house and they treated me as one of their own, quizzing me about my grades in school and kindly keeping us all in line. Steve was always quick with a joke, and already a good athlete and a good student at a young age. His older brother Dave and sister Sue were several years older, so Steve really operated as the oldest sibling for his three younger brothers. Despite his confidence around us, when he was around people from outside the group, he withdrew and became very shy.

Greg Capper, *Neighbor, now Women's Basketball Coach at Whitefish Bay High School*

We always had a conglomerate of guys playing in the street of the 5400 block of Kent Avenue, or someone's backyard, or the playground at nearby Lydell Elementary School. I was the oldest by several years, so I served as the de facto Pied Piper, but with some sort of ball rather than a flute. We were crazy for sports and we were always pulling together some sort of pickup game or physical activity. I remember Steve as a quiet study, but an intelligent leader. One summer we organized a three-on-three basketball league, and he was our Commissioner, while I followed my natural instincts and became Head Coach.

Even after everyone left for college we would still meet up with our gang of guys to play basketball, which by then had become our sport of choice. We would talk the

Lydell School janitor Ray into letting us in the gym so we could shoot hoops until we got kicked out.

Jack Bleier, *High School Coach and Teacher*

Despite the "all American boy" he appeared to be, Steve really was a somewhat quiet kind of kid who did not challenge authority. That is who Steve really was, even though he had many reasons to see himself as someone who was at least a bit special. That attitude clearly came from his parents. Jack and Mag were among the finest parents I have known in Whitefish Bay. Jack was a coach and teacher in the same school district. Both were strongly supportive of teachers and coaches who worked with their children. They were middle class, kind, humble, and as nice as they come. That was the Hirst family in a nutshell—hardworking, respectful and humble—instilled in them by some very caring parents.

Susan "Sue" Hirst, *Sister*

When Steve was born, he was doted on by my mom and dad, as well as Dave and I and our friends. He was the oldest of a large group of cousins that would be born in quick succession after him, to our mother's siblings. I think he got a good start with feeling like he could do anything, because whenever he did anything, there were plenty of us to admire it, encourage him, or imitate him. I adored him from the very beginning. What nine-year-old doesn't love a darling baby to dress up, hold and play with?!

With all of the kids in the neighborhood, no one thought of themselves as better than, or in any way more special than anyone else, and that included Steve. For those of us who watched him grow, we did realize that there was something about his personality, his work ethic, his sense of humor, his intelligence, and athletic ability that came together in a way that made us feel that he could accomplish anything he put his mind to. None of us were surprised by his success, and all of us were stunned by the fateful accident.

The Christmas before Steve was transferred to Alaska, he, Susan, and the girls came to Milwaukee. We had a terrific time. One day, Steve and I took the four cousins sledding;

his two girls, along with my two girls. We departed from Mom's Mequon residence. I'll never forget Steve's caution in the car. He would not back out of her driveway until each of the girls was clicked in their respective seatbelt. He explained how important it was that everyone always wear their seatbelt. When we arrived at the park, he showed a mix of caution and risk-taking as we all flew down the hills on the sleds we had brought. He loved the speed and thrill of flying down the hill, but also made everyone aware of where the trees, bumps, and possible hazards were.

When I heard, just two weeks later, that he had been in a terrible car accident, I could not forget the day we went sledding. The fact that he had been in a car accident, while going the speed limit, and wearing his seatbelt could not have been more ironic. He was assigned to Alaska to fly one of the fastest planes in the world, and he was in a car accident, exercising all reasonable caution. We all continue to admire his strength, hard work, sense of humor and determination that could not be taken from him, even by a tragic car accident.

Heading down the court. *Photo by Tom Corcoran*

BASKETBALL AND SPORTS

The competitive spirit I discovered at our summer cottage and in the neighborhood with my brothers and friends carried over to the court for me. One of my early mentors, my brother Dave, had instilled in me the belief that hard work, loyalty and dedication were the building blocks of success. I brought that attitude to sports and played virtually every game, every season, all year. In the spring and summer, it was track and baseball. In the fall and winter, I played football and basketball. I went to sports camps for each of the sports. That kept me busy and helped me become the best I could be. Whether it was hitting a wicked curve ball or shooting hoops, I learned to compete at a higher level.

I soon discovered that of all the sports, I loved basketball the most. For hours on end I practiced my foul shots, swishing balls through the hoop in our driveway and at the cottage. Even though I wasn't fast and I couldn't jump high either, basketball seemed to come naturally to me and I honed my talent with seemingly endless practice drills to work on dribbling and passing. To raise my level of play, I constantly played against older guys, kids who had already made names for themselves as stars on the local high school team. They told me what I already knew: Steve was my name and basketball was my game.

I think sports also helped me overcome my shyness. It helped me establish my identity in a town that packed the stands at local sporting events. I'd spend a lot of time at Greg Capper's house shooting hoops for hours at a time. Greg was several grades ahead of me, but very generous with his time and advice.

In fifth grade, our basketball coach arranged a game against a college women's team. Chris Riordan likes to tell people I single-handedly won that game. When I was in sixth or seventh grade, I scored thirty-three points in one half and dominated the opposing team. Soon, I was holding my own against college players who let me play with them while they were home from school.

Despite my love of basketball, I was aware of my limitations. I was six feet tall. I couldn't jump. But at least I was slow! I knew I was a long shot to become a basketball star. But I worked on anticipating defenses and passing the ball. I knew the description of an ideal guard: the guy who does a lot of the playmaking and setting things up for the scorers on the team. Eventually my hard work paid off. I had made a name for myself in Whitefish Bay with both players my age and with the older players in the area.

We had some amazing seasons with Coach Bleier and Coach Thielke. In his first seasons at Whitefish Bay, Jack Bleier wasn't that much older than we were, but he ran a tight ship.

By the time I was a junior in high school, scouts from basketball powerhouses like Northwestern and Marquette took notice of my potential. But, after breaking my wrist my senior season, the recruiters stopped coming around. It wasn't my only injury that year. In the spring, while running the high hurdles, I suffered a stress fracture in my leg. I was devastated. I had pinned all my hopes and dreams on playing college basketball and suddenly, I had no options. I had not thought about what I would do if I was not going to play college ball.

OTHER PERSPECTIVES

Dick Stadler, *High School Friend*

I first got to know Steve through Saturday basketball league in grade school. We ended up participating in many sports together in high school and we had some amazing times. The best season was when our Junior Varsity team went 17–1. Steve was definitely the best player on the team, and I was most certainly not. I like to say we balanced both ends of the bench. But he never made me feel that way—we had a great team. It was all about the love of the game.

Jack Bleier, *High School Coach and Teacher*

I first met Steve when I was coaching the boys' sophomore basketball team. Steve was on the freshman team at the time, but I got to see him play a lot. Athletically, Steve was slightly above average, but not overly gifted. Steve would go on to be a decent football player and hurdler. But his special gift was basketball.

He was certainly adequate defensively, but his basketball IQ and his offensive prowess were unusually high. He had a great outside shot, handled the ball in a way where he always saw the whole floor well, and had a knack for going to the basket and playing inside where he just made things happen. As an offensive player, Steve was certainly a talent.

The next year, Steve played for me on the sophomore team. At that point, I did not really know him well. He seemed to be the "fair haired" boy in his sophomore class. But he had a very quiet demeanor. I wasn't sure if he was just a "quiet kid," or aloof. And

Mike Brand, David Farley, me up in the air, and Coaches Morken and Bleier.
Photo by Tom Corcoran.

though he was surrounded by some pretty good athletes, it was clear that Steve was the best basketball player of the group.

There was one incident I remember vividly. It was one of the first practices we had that year. Steve was handling the ball on the open floor and the defender pushed a little toward the sideline, but Steve made a behind-the-back pass before going out of bounds. It was on time, on target. But I stopped the practice and got all over him. I believed in solid fundamentals, not style. Though what he had done could be rationalized by the predicament he had found himself in, I wanted to make two things clear. First, no fancy stuff like behind-the-back dribbles or passes, which were not common anyways in those days. Second, no matter how good Steve was, he was not going to be treated as a "prima donna." Steve was not going to get special treatment. This was a "team" operation.

After getting after him, I watched for his reaction. He didn't roll his eyes. He didn't back-talk. He simply acknowledged me with, "Yes Coach, I hear you." In that moment I learned a lot about Steve.

We had a wonderful basketball season when Steve was a sophomore. We won our first fourteen games that year and finished 17–1. We were very much a team. Everyone worked together. The next year Steve was the lone junior who started on the varsity team. We finished second in the conference to South Milwaukee, a team that finished the year as State Champions with an undefeated season. Whitefish Bay gave South Milwaukee their toughest game of the year, ignoring their home-court advantage. Steve was voted second team all-conference, a very big deal for a high school junior.

The next year Steve made it through the football season injury-free. But during the first basketball game, he drove to the basket, was fouled hard, and suffered a broken wrist when he fell. The team had an awful season. His return at the end of the season was too late. Steve found that most of the college scouts had lost interest.

He was in a love affair with basketball, but with his senior season washed out, he was stood up for the big dance. In those years there was no summer AAU basketball where coaches could assess his talents. To make matters worse, the head basketball coach was fired and did not seem interested in helping Steve find a school where he could play.

USAFA graduation photo, 1981.

CHAPTER SIX

ADJUSTING TO CADET LIFE

Only one college scout had stuck by me. Sam Peshut, of the United States Air Force Academy, came by our house and talked with me and my parents. To our surprise, the Academy was still interested. My parents and I thought the broken wrist had completely dashed my hopes for any college basketball experience.

The military academies gave extra attention to sports ability, which gave me some priority over other applicants. Peshut pointed out that basketball was only one of the reasons I was considered for the Academy. I would get a chance to make the basketball team, but the Academy wanted me because of my academic achievements. They thought I would make an excellent cadet and Air Force officer.

After talking to my local AFA liaison officer, I decided to pursue an appointment. I prepared for the Physical Fitness Test, and took it a few times at the Milwaukee Air National Guard Unit. I also took the SAT a couple of times before I left for the Academy. It took more than once to get my score up where I thought it should be. So, once I decided on this direction, I was suddenly busy testing and retesting.

I had never spent much time away from home, family, and friends. Not knowing what to expect, I packed up and headed west for Colorado Springs and the sprawling Academy near the base of Pikes Peak. What I found was an alien environment.

It was 1977. From the start, I didn't feel that I belonged as a cadet at the Air Force Academy, but I stayed anyway. Despite my disciplined habits in sports and studying, I had a pretty immature attitude about the realities of being a cadet. The commanding officers gave us many orders and approved the Squadron Policies and Wing Regulations, which were all about approval and disapproval of just about everything. There were even rules about clothing for all cadet activities.

Until that time, clothes for me meant clean jeans and a shirt, and plenty of athletic attire. Now there were very specific rules for cadet military uniforms for classroom activities, outdoor activities, indoor activities and military training, such as parades and inspections. There was special cold weather gear, even athletic wear like swimsuits. All of these things were approved and inspected by many officers, and everything had to be perfectly clean and correctly worn.

I finally started to feel pretty good about being there by the end of my freshman year. And, when I started feeling better, things started getting better, like academics and basketball.

I first met Gregg Popovich when basketball season started at the Academy. Popo, as we called him, was an assistant coach on the Varsity squad. Well, we called him Coach when he could hear us, but Popo between the players when he wasn't around. Since I played JV, and he was coaching Varsity, we didn't interact much in the beginning. Plus, I was too wrapped up in what was happening to me to pay attention to someone else.

Between classes, practice, and the new world of orders and regulations, I had more than enough to keep me busy. Popo and I rarely talked, and we didn't know much about each other. I couldn't wait to fly for the Air Force, and I'm sure he couldn't wait to get out of the Air Force and pursue his coaching dreams. By the time I advanced to Varsity, he had already moved on to coach at a civilian college, and I never got the chance to play for him.

I grew to admire his coaching skills when watching him coach the Varsity players. He saw any mistake as an opportunity to help a player, or make the team even better. I was fortunate to see film and video of his own playing days at the Academy, and could see he had the same attitude when he was a player. He impressed me with his approach to every member of the team. I remember that he was always fair to me as a player, even though I never had a chance of being a star, and both he and I knew it. He always treated people fairly no matter their playing ability. His personality made him liked and admired by everyone. The coaches and the players on the Academy team really respected him.

I would like to say I could always tell he was bound for an NBA coaching job, but I had no idea. He coached at a small college, Cal Poly Pomona, I think, as his first coaching job after leaving the AFA in the late 70s. Kurt Herbst, a friend of mine from the Academy and the basketball team, and I went and watched Popovich coach one game in California. Following that coaching job, I'm not sure what he did, but I'm sure it involved pursuing a coaching career in the NBA.

Later, during my recovery from the accident, he played a huge role in keeping me in therapy, helping me financially and ensuring I had good exercise equipment. When he heard about my injuries, we began e-mailing each other, and we talked on the phone. His generosity touched and amazed me. Just talking to him was probably my greatest inspiration. I will never be able to truly repay him for his support and friendship. They are priceless.

Some say good guys finish last. Coach Pop is living proof that good guys not only win, but they do it with integrity and style. He has had a distinguished coaching career. As head coach of the San Antonio Spurs, he always has a few tickets waiting for me when they play the Denver Nuggets. I am proud and honored to call him my friend.

I sat the bench my junior and senior year, more than I did my sophomore season. Even so, I enjoyed basketball season. It helped keep my interest in staying on at the Academy. The longer I was there, the more I knew the routine and understood the policies and regulations, so day-to-day life got easier. Well, maybe I didn't understand everything, but I had learned to live with the rules without them being the focus of my very existence.

There were still times when I was ready to get the heck out of the Academy. But by

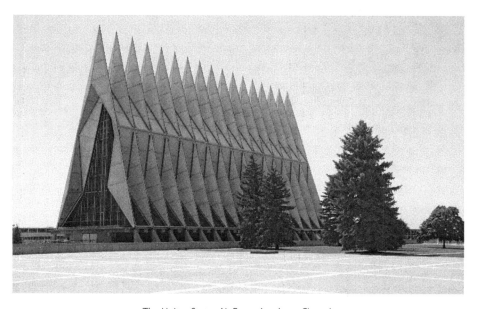

The Unites States Air Force Academy Chapel.

the time my four years were completed, I had come to enjoy it enough to remain an additional year in Colorado. I was asked to teach at the Air Force Preparatory School, helping high school graduates get ready for their freshman year of college academics at the Academy. I taught calculus, and was also assistant coach for the men's basketball team under the head coach, Rich Gugat. He was a great individual who had a hilarious sense of humor. I wish I could remember the specifics, but I do remember he made me laugh. Anyway, remaining at the Academy after graduation worked for me, as I had another good reason to stay around.

Of the many new things the Academy introduced me to, certainly the most beautiful was a younger cadet named Susan Roth. Susan was from Pueblo, Colorado, and her parents were teachers at a high school there, an hour's drive south of the Academy. Our family upbringing had similarities. She was two years behind me, and we often ended up hanging out with the same group of cadets. There have always been strict rules about dating at the Academy, especially in the first year.

As cadets, we were paid a small amount monthly. Sometimes, I felt like we were getting ripped off, and other times I'd be thrilled with the payment. We were very imaginative with money because we had to be. Susan remembers our first official date as the time I paid for her ticket when a bunch of us cadets went out for a movie.

I had started my financial planning with a guy named Bill Zint. I believed it was a smart thing to do, and told Susan if we got married we'd be saving for the future. Notice my subtle approach to the idea of marriage. I knew by then she was the one to build a life with, and had started thinking about our future together. At that point, we thought all things would keep rising in value. We kept contributing, and that turned out to be a good thing.

Susan was, and still is, very beautiful. Her green eyes, high cheekbones, and her kindness and sense of humor, really did a number on me. She tells me I sent her a homemade Valentine while I was out of town, and suggested she pick out a ring.

That must have done it. We were married on June 18, 1983, a month after she graduated from the Academy.

OTHER PERSPECTIVES

Jack Bleier, *High School Coach and Teacher*

That spring of his senior year in high school, Steve and I identified Northwestern as a possible place for him to continue playing ball. I wrote a letter on his behalf, but nothing came of that. Then, the opportunity to play at the Air Force Academy appeared, and the rest is history. Steve played there, but did not see a lot of playing time. At the time, the Air Force Academy had height restrictions and their tallest player was six feet, six inches. Probably as a result of that, their coach, Hank Egan, ran a team that played tough defense and a disciplined half-court offense, certainly not tailored to Steve's game. Though Steve could play defense, his offensive talents were more geared to an open floor type of offensive team. Nonetheless, it was what it was.

Still, basketball had led him to the Air Force Academy. He ended up flying F-15s, quite an elite occupation. He did some flying during the first Gulf War. He would later explain to me the great amount of individual preparation time that was needed to fly for just one hour and how physically exhausting one hour of flying could be. So this was special. Not many people got to fly these wonderful aircraft. Later on, I heard stories of how Steve, when he was an officer, would play as much basketball as possible with troops on the base. He gained quite a reputation on base for his basketball talents. Basketball and competing were just part of Steve's DNA.

Jeff Wilkerson, *Pilot*

It is customary at the Air Force Academy to change cadet squadrons every couple of years. This provides for more cross-pollination amongst the cadet wing. I was assigned to the 37th Squadron my junior year. As I moved in, I met Susan Roth, a swimmer for the Academy's varsity women's swim team, in the hallway. Over the next two years we developed a fast friendship that allowed us to open up about ourselves and our lives. Susan had been dating Steve for a couple of years already by the time I met her. So, when we talked about relationships, Susan always referred to Steve. The irony is that I had never met Steve, nor would I meet him the entire time I was at the Academy. For me, I won't say that Steve was "the other guy" that was with the girl I liked, but he was a mystery figure that was very much part of my friend Susan's life.

Bobby Renaud, *Air Force Academy Friend and Pilot*

Steve and I first met at the Academy. I played football, and he played basketball, so cadet life had us pretty tightly scheduled. We really got to know each other better the year we both stayed on to coach at the AFA after graduation, as graduate assistants. I was a freshman defensive coach for football, and I had always known Steve as a good basketball player, even though he didn't see much action on the varsity team. I had no idea he could play football.

We organized a flag football team that would play other base units. We were stacked with talent. Bobby Bledsoe and Todd Anderson had both played football, while Al Pegorio was a decathlete, and Steve had basketball. For intramural football, I was the quarterback, and Steve was one of the wide receivers. All I had to do was throw the ball up, and Steve would go get it. I don't know if it was him translating his basketball moves to the football field, but he was so elusive. Guys just couldn't catch him. We ended up competing for the Air Force Flag Football championship.

I also remember being so poor that first year after graduation. Date night for our ladies was hanging out at the apartment complex where we were living, where they handed out free popcorn and showed movies. Or we would play board games. Whatever, we did, Steve always had that easygoing smile.

Susan Hirst, *Wife*

As a fourth-classman or freshman in the USAFA's 28th squadron and an intercollegiate swimmer, I had little time or interest in knowing my upperclass squadron mates. That said, it was not possible to remain completely anonymous or unaware of those around me. Steve was one of the upperclassman that drew my attention. Though I didn't have any real contact with him, apart from perhaps an occasional greeting in hallways, he was noticeable because of his calm bearing, soft spoken but powerful presence, and, if I recall correctly, really long legs and rather short, 1980s-style, light blue terry shorts. Weird.

Late in the spring, when the taboo against upperclassmen and freshmen socializing was lifted, Steve and I began a quirky little ritual that in retrospect was our innocent way of testing the waters before opening ourselves to a relationship. Steve, a fan of the television show M.A.S.H., would go to the squadron TV room each evening. I'd head to the drinking fountain in the hall where we'd meet. From there, I'd join him and his friends for the half-hour show. A couple months later I joined the same group of guys to go see the movie "The Rose," a strange movie for a group of guys to choose. Only after Steve bought my ticket to the movie did I know we were on a date. Understated. Some summer dating and a bit of time apart and meeting other people was the dance before we made a permanent connection the following October. A date then was the beginning of what is now more than thirty years together.

I had no doubt that Steve and I would marry. We'd been talking about our future for some time. Still, I'd been disappointed when the engagement ring I'd expected at Christmas turned out to be a racquetball racquet. In February, while Steve was traveling through Europe playing basketball with a US military team competing against military teams from other countries represented in SHAPE, Supreme Headquarters Allied Powers Europe, I was a junior or 2-degree (second classman) in the 37th squadron at USAFA. Being apart for Valentine's Day dampens the celebration, but receiving a crayon-drawn Valentine on yellow construction paper, which contained a proposal for marriage shocked me to the core. Surprise! Heck.

Dunking Bobby Renaud after his first solo flight at Williams Air Force Base.

PILOT TRAINING AND MY NEW FAMILY

Following the year of post-graduate teaching and coaching, I left the Academy for Arizona for my year-long undergraduate pilot training program at Williams Air Force Base, commonly called Willy. Susan joined me in Phoenix after her graduation and our wedding. By the time she got there, I had completed my flight training and had started working for the Air Force as an instructor pilot at Willy. I taught students, like I had been the year before, how to fly their first jet, the T-37. The term used for my position was First Assignment Instructor Pilot, or FAIP. It wasn't a coveted job, but I was determined to make the most of it.

Our newlywed years in Arizona were happy years. Susan's job was on the other side of Phoenix as an auditor at Luke Air Force Base, but we were home together most evenings. I was enjoying my flying and I loved teaching others how to fly. Susan and I could spend our free time together, and our two paychecks permitted us to start saving for the future. What was not to like?!

The future came fast. Our beautiful daughter Stephanie Noelle was born on July 5, 1985, at the Luke Air Force Base Hospital. And we wasted no time bringing a sister for her into our lives. The equally beautiful Stacey Christine was born the following year at Williams Air Force Base Hospital on December 20. We loved those early years with our girls, but I recall how hard it was on us to leave them when we left for work in the morning. That meant daycare, babysitters or the nursery for both Stephanie and Stacey. I could tell the girls missed us during those hours, because they were so happy when we came to get them every day.

With the family together, and getting paid to do something I enjoyed so much, I really was on top of the world in every way. Prior to that, my most difficult years were adjusting to the Academy. Approaching the end of my three-year FAIP assignment, I was finally considered a good, solid pilot, and I was chosen to go to Okinawa, Japan to fly the best fighter plane in the world: the F-15 Eagle. Best of all, Susan and the girls would go with me for our next adventure.

OTHER PERSPECTIVES

Bobby Renaud, *Air Force Academy Friend and Pilot*

Pilot training with Steve those years in Arizona was so much fun. He was instructing on the T-37 and I was on the T-38. We were both young married couples, and we did a lot together, playing any sport we could think up, flying, going boating, and just hanging out.

Steve loved to organize "kamikaze parties," where we would sit around the pool with

Acting cool by the pool while at Willie.

snacks and drinks, acting like pilots. It was so hot, and the water in the pool was too hot, so we would dump about twenty bags of ice into it, just to get the temperature down below our own.

That same apartment complex had tennis courts, and Steve and I would conduct these insane five-setters in 120-degree heat. During the breaks, we would have a beer in one hand and a Gatorade in the other. The heat didn't seem to faze him—he could spend hours instructing, playing hoops or tennis, always with that smile.

Tom Hogan, *Pilot*

Nobody wants a T-37 instructor assignment at the end of pilot training. Nobody. I was ready to drown myself on assignment night. I had been sure I was bound for a front-line fighter in the combat Air Force. For weeks, the T-38 instructors had been dropping hints to my classmates who were likely to stay behind in the training world as FAIPs, First Assignment Instructor Pilots at Willy. Willy was Williams Air Force Base. Comments like, "Hey, at least you're not stuck at Del Rio for three years. Have you checked out that new subdivision in Mesa?" Or just a whistle that sounded like the slow startup of the engines on a T-37.

Some classmates were realists and grudgingly volunteered for FAIP purgatory in hopes of a better assignment after those years. Realism wasn't my thing, though. I'd received no hints of impending FAIPdom. After doing well in pilot training, I knew an appropriate reward would follow. So, I was shocked when, on stage in front of my whole class and all our IPs (instructor pilots), I opened my assignment envelope and read "T-37, Willy." After a few seconds of private humiliation, I scratched my assignment onto the chalkboard, causing the rest of the class, who had been cheering each assignment, to groan in collective disbelief. I stumbled back to my chair, tried to disappear, and then bolted out of the room as soon as all the slots were awarded. I tried every escape from that assignment. No luck.

The Air Force was sending me back to the minors. In four short weeks, I would say goodbye to my classmates, who were off to fly hot new aircraft around the world. I would remain in the school house and downshift from the sleek, supersonic T-38 to the plodding, no-AC, no G-suit, side-by-side-seated Tweet. Three years in the desert heat, hoping students wouldn't throw up on me.

After pilot training, it took six months to relearn the Tweet and learn to teach. I returned from IP school at Randolph Air Force Base, in Texas, convinced I'd be the greatest Tweet instructor Willy had ever seen. All I had to do, I thought, was apply the techniques I'd learned at Randolph and dazzle the students with my hands-on skills.

The T-37 squadron assigned me and two of my Academy classmates, Kurt Schake and Nora Vick, to Scatpack flight. Scatpack's senior IPs were three bad-asses: Doug Dunbar, Greg Grover, and Steve Hirst. The Scatpack flight commander, Rob Davies, was officially in charge, but Doug, Greg, and Steve were the soul of the operation. New instructors were considered somewhat like apprentices until they'd taught a class of new students through all phases of training. So, Rob assigned Kurt, Nora, and me a big brother, or "buddy IP" (BIP), to guide us through the apprenticeship and help us bridge the considerable gap between Randolph's learning lab and Willy's real world.

My BIP was Steve. What I found from Doug, Greg, and Steve was that I had a lot to learn about flying the Tweet and even more to learn about teaching. Students consistently rated Doug, Greg, and Steve the best instructors. And all three were great pilots. Scatpack was no minor-league team. I needed much practice before I'd be playing at their level. Steve was the IP I wanted to be. Nothing fazed him. Nothing surprised him. He anticipated his students' mistakes. He was generous with praise. He was gracious when his students flew poorly. I never saw him blow up at a student, even if he was on his third sortie of the day in the Arizona summer heat. He seemed to like the job and thought it was important.

On my very first instructional ride, my student tried to land without lowering the gear—unbelievable. The Randolph IPs told us these things would happen, but I wasn't expecting it so soon. The Randolph IPs also insisted any attempted gear-up landing meant a failed grade. No question. So, when I returned to the flight room after landing, I pulled Steve and Greg into Rob's office and told them I was about to bust the student. They listened to my argument and asked how the rest of the ride had gone. "Not bad," I said. Steve asked, "So apart from the gear-up thing, the student did alright? No other safety issues? He wasn't flying around with his head up his ass?" No, I replied. Greg and Steve looked at each other and laughed.

"Uh, yeah. Well, you're right, this is a big deal. And, if you want to bust the kid, you certainly have grounds, and we'll back you up. But here's the difference between the real world and what you learned at Randolph." They had a point. So, I passed the kid on that sortie, but gave him a severe debrief. I emphasized he'd used his only freebee in that area. The lesson stuck, the kid did well for the rest of T-37s, graduated from pilot training, and went out into the combat Air Force. And Steve had given me my first lesson in judgment and discretion, something I hadn't learned at Randolph.

For four months, Steve guided me through that initial class. I'd teach a student for three sorties, and then Steve would evaluate that same student on the fourth. Occasionally, Steve and I flew formation, cross-country, instruments, and nights in the same airplane, and I'd walk away thinking, "Damn, this guy's a good stick." When he cleared me off at the end of the BIP program, I was a much better teacher than the newbie who'd strutted into Scatpack fresh out of Randolph.

After T-37s, I would see the world, fight the wars, and fly the best airplanes in the combat Air Force. But I would never again have the daily job satisfaction of my T-37 FAIP tour. Nor would I ever have a cooler big brother. After Steve left Willy, I wouldn't see him again for seventeen years.

Jeff Wilkerson, *Pilot*

I was destined to cross paths with the Hirsts throughout my time in the Air Force. My first assignment was to Williams Air Force Base in Chandler, AZ. I showed up in June, 1983, ready to conquer the brilliant blue skies of the desert southwest. As it turns out, Susan and Steve, newly married, were also stationed at Williams, or Willy. Susan was commuting to Luke Air Force Base across town, while Steve was a T-37 instructor pilot at Williams. I don't think I made too big an impression on Steve when we met. Some young gun student pilot that knows his new wife may have been thought of more as competition than a prospective lifelong friend. Since my roommates at the Academy were also at Willy, the five of us did find time to get together a couple of times during the year. Steve, at this point, was more of a larger than life character to me. Heck, he could even recite the spin recovery procedure for the T-37 backwards. I was probably a little stand-offish as I spent time with Susan and Steve, afraid that I might look foolish to Steve, the T-37 instructor pilot. I wouldn't see Susan and Steve for the next few years.

Susan Hirst, *Wife*

The day I was married I was ready to be a mother. Steve however was not quite convinced fatherhood was in his near-term plans. As it turns out, we split the difference. Just a few weeks after our second wedding anniversary, Stephanie was born. Steve was immediately smitten. When we brought her into our home, Steve was nearly overwhelmed. He placed her carrier down on a counter, stepped back, and although

Susan and Steve—newlyweds.

I don't recall his exact words, suffice it to say, he marveled that this amazing creation was in his home and was his child. Our lives were immediately richer.

Steve was an excellent daddy. I nursed Stephanie for six months and, to do his part, Steve would wake to her cries, change her, and bring his baby girl to me. Without fail, she was his focus every evening after work. Most nights Steve and Stephanie would go for a drive that served to lull her to sleep. Before she was a year old, he decided he needed to extend their travels together and show her off to family and friends in Wisconsin. Off they went for a week-long daddy-daughter jaunt. By this time baby #2 was on the way. Steve was convinced, and freely shared the fact, that he would not be able to love another child as he loved Stephanie. Wrong!

Off we go!

CHAPTER EIGHT

THE WILD BLUE YONDER AND MY AIR FORCE FAMILY

The F-15 was a great jet in every way: better visibility from the cockpit than previous fighters, a better radar for detecting adversaries, more and better missiles, and more maneuverable in a turning fight. It would have been easy to feel a bit of personal superiority in mastering the F-15, but it didn't take too long for me to appreciate that learning to fly the jet was just the start of a long learning curve to being a good fighter pilot. I had a long way to go.

I was finally getting my opportunity to serve on what we loosely referred to as "the pointy end of the sword," versus being in an academic or training role. My initial assignment in the F-15 was to the 67th Fighter Squadron at Kadena Air Base, Okinawa. Little did I know it was one of the best fighter squadrons in the Air Force. At the time, I was just happy to be there and was busy trying to learn all that was expected of me.

Fortunately, the Air Force needed auditors at Kadena as well, so we were able to go to Okinawa as a family. It was a three-year assignment. Too short for me as an F-15 pilot and loving the flying as I did. Too long for a family living on a small island a long way from relatives and friends. No Target, no Home Depot and no Toys R Us.

It was there I earned my pilot handle, "Blaster." Maybe it was not my finest moment, better categorized as "a learning experience," but the event stuck with me and I have been called Blaster by my Air Force friends ever since.

There is no typical day for an F-15 pilot. Those taking the early flights would start before dawn. Briefings usually began two hours prior to takeoff. Four aircraft were a frequent training formation, sometimes just two, and occasionally multiple formations of four, one pilot per plane.

The preflight briefing would cover the weather, our individual aircraft assignments and who was acting on defense and offense that day, the objectives of the training, tactics to be used, rules and limitations governing the flight and how we would recover to the base. Then the opposing sides of the training exercise would split into separate rooms and come up with a plan to outdo the other side during the simulated air combat portion of the flight. Then we would put on our flight gear: an anti-G suit to keep blood from flooding our legs and lower guts during hard turns, a harness to secure the pilot to the aircraft-mounted personal parachutes (which we hoped not to use), and a helmet with an oxygen mask, microphone, earphones and sun visor.

A short flight was under an hour. Long flights were over two hours. Most were in between. Takeoff, climb-out and the early setups for the maneuvers were typically routine and uneventful. Until that point in a flight, things went pretty much as planned. But when simulated fighting started, it was anything but structured, easy or routine. Doing well was a product of knowledge, discipline, having learned from mistakes and success, trust in each other, teamwork and more. It took two to three flights a week to retain proficiency, more to get better.

The debriefing of each flight was often longer than the flight itself. Every detail was discussed, in order to learn from any mistakes and reinforce what worked. On a good day, we would fly once, then spend time with our additional duties assigned to run the squadron. On a great day, we would fly more than once.

Much of our flying was in the overwater areas near the island of Okinawa. At other times, we would deploy to mainland Japan, Korea, the Philippines, and once even to Australia, for training opportunities with other air forces, or with American pilots stationed in those countries. Deployments were a way of life and a welcome change from the routine of Okinawa. We deployed two to three weeks every other month or so, at least a deployment each quarter. As pilots, we looked forward to testing our skills against others. We used the concentrated time together on deployments to form stronger personal bonds through off-duty sports, meals together, workouts at the gym, and an occasional visit to a local bar.

Deployments were not as popular with our family members. It was tough for them being on an island without many of the conveniences of life back home. But it was harder when the squadron was deployed, leaving spouses and kids to deal with the issues that would surface. Boredom came easily to many. One person's problems would become everyone's problems. Most were missing someone back in the United States. Families coped by coming together, spending more time with other families in the squadron and supporting each other as needed.

I know separations were hard on Stephanie and Stacey because they learned early how to tell I was discussing an upcoming deployment, or cross-country trip. I would have to be gone overnight, or sometimes several nights as part of my flying duties, and it didn't take long for the girls to recognize the lingo and react negatively to any mention of me going. The girls also soon recognized the letters "T," "D," and "Y." That meant Susan was being sent somewhere for a few weeks to do an audit at another base, TDY was the acronym for Temporary Duty. It was tough to see their little faces crumple when we had to travel, but it was what Susan and I had signed up to do.

One couple kept a sign in their kitchen that read, "Home is Where the Air Force Sends Us," making light of the control we forfeited by serving. The bonds of friendship formed here and in later assignments would return to us in the years following my accident in ways I never imagined.

The assignments we had after leaving Okinawa were also good because we were able to keep the family together, Susan and I being assigned to the same bases at the same times. The first was at Luke Air Force Base back in Phoenix, where I was able to continue flying the F-15. Too many of my peers were being reassigned to nonflying jobs or to other aircraft after Kadena. I felt lucky.

Band of brothers with the F-15 Eagle.

Later we were moved to Langley Air Force Base in Virginia for my first staff tour. It wasn't something most pilots looked forward to, but we understood the Air Force needed experienced fliers in staff jobs too and we also had to vacate cockpits so the younger pilots could build flying time as I had. In both places, our experiences were similar to our time in Okinawa: more good people, more bonds of friendship, and continued expansion of the Air Force family that would later help us through hard times.

By the end of my staff tour in Virginia, I was hoping for a supervisory position in a flying squadron, hopefully a fighter squadron, and ideally an F-15 squadron. Luck happened! I was off to fly the F-15 Eagle at Elmendorf Air Base in Alaska. The timing was near perfect. Susan would be able to attend her Air Force intermediate-level academic schooling at the Air University in Alabama, while I refreshed my F-15 skills at a base in Florida. We were even close enough for the family to spend some weekends together. Following her schooling, the plan was for Susan and the girls to join me in Alaska, about the time I would be getting comfortable in my new role.

I wouldn't have done anything differently. But I never dreamed that I would be uniquely grounded within a month after arriving at Elmendorf AFB in Alaska. Making a very bad situation worse, Susan and the girls were thousands of miles away in Alabama.

OTHER PERSPECTIVES

Susan Hirst, *Wife*

If Stephanie owned Steve's heart, Stacey owned his soul. Two girls just seventeen months apart in age with working parents and literally oceans away from family support, our three years in Okinawa, Japan bound our little family for all time. Steve worked hard to do as much parenting as possible. He and I would meet most afternoons at the child care center on base and each would take one child home. Because I traveled regularly to both Guam and Tokyo, Japan for as much as three weeks at a time, Steve got the opportunity to do a good amount of single parenting. Not an easy task but I think he relished the time with his girls. Fortunately our Air Force careers allowed that to continue, as we moved together from Japan to Arizona to Virginia. Steve actively parented and played with his girls as well as their friends and cousins.

Family gatherings were sure to have Steve entertaining the youngsters on water, sand, and snow. In the gym and on the field he coached and cheered their sports and arts. Stacey went an extra step and embraced Steve's music choices. Together they rocked with The Allman Brothers on Friday nights in our Virginia family room. A proud Papa, most definitely!

David Hayes, *former commander, 67th Fighter Squadron, Okinawa*

I laughed when I read Steve wrote he was considered, ". . . a good, solid pilot . . . ," and that's what led to his assignment to the F-15. You have to know the degree of his humility to appreciate just how much of an understatement that is. Although the F-15 had been operational in the Air Force for about ten years by then, there was nothing average or just "solid" about the young pilots being assigned to fly them, and especially not Steve. In every case, they were selected from the best of their peers—top in academics, top in their flying training classes, top of their annual officer performance reports, and so on.

Consider, it wasn't easy to earn entry to the Air Force Academy. Once there, the competition was tough to merit a pilot training slot upon graduation. At pilot training, tougher still, with only a handful at the top of each class being designated "fighter qualified." The pilot training schools picked their instructors, or FAIPs, from this group. Very few FAIPs ever went on to fly fighters, fewer still to fly the F-15.

No, there was little "solid" about Steve Hirst other than his athletic build. It was apparent early after his arrival at the squadron in Okinawa that he was talented, mature, and a leader far beyond his years. He'd just never say that about himself.

Howie Chandler, *General, USAF, Ret.*

The 67th TFS was deployed to Osan Air base in the Republic of Korea for a flying exercise on the Korean Peninsula. If I remember correctly, I was Steve's flight lead for a mission that scrambled a two-ship of F-15s from Osan to a nearby training area for dissimilar air combat training with F-16s. Always the conscientious wingman, Steve was intent on being timely and ready to taxi with his flight lead. As we pulled out of the chocks (our individual parking places), I looked back to see Steve ready to go. However, as he made his first turn out of parking, rather than reducing his power as was the standard, he left the throttles well above idle. Thus, he blew everything the crew chief had positioned next to his aircraft—intake covers, chocks, ladder, tool box, fire bottle, the assistant crew chief, etc., across the ramp in a wind storm that required nearby crew chiefs' considerable effort to sort, reclaim and reposition their aircraft support gear. Needless to say, when we returned from the mission, the ground crews greeted Steve with a less-than-enthusiastic welcome. Following a debriefing that included a discussion of power management on the ground, Steve apologized to all the crew chiefs—a testimony to the type of officer he was. That said, his performance did not go unnoticed in the next naming session where "Blaster" was unanimously selected by his squadron mates to be his tac call sign!

Jeff Wilkerson, *Pilot*

The Air Force is really quite a small community. The fighter community is even smaller. In 1988 I showed up at Kadena Air Force Base to fly the greatest fighter in the world, the F-15. I was assigned to the 67th Fighter Squadron. The story of the 67th Fighter Squadron, the Fighting Cocks, is a book in itself. Without knowing it, I had been assigned to the best fighter squadron in the U.S. Air Force. One of the major players in the Cocks, as we referred to ourselves, was Captain Steve Hirst. Yep, I was based with Susan and Steve again. Now they had two baby girls and a house on the base. Meanwhile, I was still a single guy ready to conquer the world. I think babies probably break down a lot of barriers. That, and flying the speed of sound on some guy's wingtip. At any rate, Steve and I finally started to have the friendship that we have today. We hung out together after a flight. Everyone loved scuba diving at Kadena for recreation, so we would go out on dive trips on the weekends. We had fantastic weekend trips in the Philippines to little resorts dotted along the Luzon coast. Of all my time in the Air Force, my three years at Kadena rate clearly the highest in terms of experience. Steve shared that great time with me. Along the way we became fast friends. I would not see Steve again for over ten years, well after the day he took on that dreaded power pole.

Kwang-ball
One of the major tasks our Kadena squadron had was to sit "alert" in Korea. We would

fly four jets to Korea from Kadena for three weeks at a time. Usually we would stage from Osan Air Base near Seoul. Due to construction at Osan, the alert location was changed to a Korean Air Force base near Kwang Ju, South Korea. Suddenly, we were in a place that was not at all like the "little America" that Okinawa represented. We were in the heart of a completely different culture that was little changed from the Korean War. The base was definitely running on a much higher readiness level for conflict with the North than we, the F-15 pilots, were used to. Due to increased tensions in town, we were asked to limit our visits there. This was an easy request to comply with since none of us spoke any Korean, and the locals spoke little or no English. So, for three weeks our lives were spent in a small dormitory with a little Commissary and cafeteria. There was a basketball court with a worn ball. This was used daily to help us combat the ennui that quickly set in while we sat around waiting to fly. Steve was definitely the champion "HORSE" player during our stay.

One day, after about a week of sitting, Blaster and I found a baseball bat and a softball. During my Academy days, one thing I learned was that when you are bored, anything can be turned into a game. In this case, a softball, a bat, and a very large concrete bunker that houses a fully loaded and armed F-15 can be turned into "Kwang-ball." The bunker, or Tab-V as we called it, had ridges or ripples on it. When a ball hit the ridges, it would go flying straight up, straight down, or any which way. Thus the game was born. Simply pitch the softball to the batter that is facing the Tab-V. Hit the ball against the concrete bunker, and watch the pitcher now scramble to catch the ball. Three flies up with a twist. It would seem like a game that could be fun for an hour or two; however, lock yourself on a Korean Air Force Base for three weeks and Kwang-ball becomes a major pastime. So Steve and I played day and night. Think Steve McQueen with his baseball in "The Great Escape". I can't understand why no one else really took to the game, but the two of us loved it. After the cover was completely ruined on the softball, we went in search of other balls. Anything we could hit against the Tab-V. So, Steve and I share a special bond in that we are still world champion Kwang-ball players.

Ron "Hobo" McNeill, *Pilot*

Blaster was the first person I met upon arriving in Okinawa in April 1988. We shared many memorable trips—taking the jets to Korea for typhoon evacuation, sitting air defense alert at Osan, combat training exercises in the Philippines, and a memorable three weeks of night flying with the Aussies in Darwin. His extremely sharp wit kept me guessing, and looking over my shoulder for his next "attack." He's one of the funniest guys I know. Went by the, "nothing is too mean, as long as it is funny," philosophy.

Being on the receiving end of Blaster's wit, my rarely effective comebacks involved comparing him to Susan—who as we all knew, was amazing. I remember Steve mentioning that she would get up in the middle of the night to, like, bake a cake or something. I readily understood everything Susan did for the family, but what was Blaster's contribution?! Susan was a full-time active duty officer, took care of two young daughters, was a beast at the gym with the body building (even competing on American Gladiator later), and she put up with Steve as well. When I made the comparison, he would let me know, "Yeah, she's pretty lucky to have me," and then grin like he was something special. The kidding was constant, except when it came to flying.

In the late '80s, there was no better place to be flying Eagles than in Okinawa. We worked long, hard hours, but we played equally hard when deployed away from our families. It helped pass the time and improved trusts and commitments between pilots—valuable to the way we fought the F-15. Away from the flying, it was a time when we pushed it up pretty hard. Blaster and Eric "Whitey" Cox were often the initiators of trouble in the name of fun. They were typically shaming me into going out. I was the finisher—never wanting to call it a night. One of those nights led to being called Hobo. What else would you call the guy who was too tired to retrieve a replacement room key, instead crawling up on his doormat to sleep out the night?!

Karen Sims, *Air Force Spouse in Okinawa*

Toward the end of my husband John's (a.k.a. José) time in the 67th TFS at Kadena AFB, Susan and Blaster transferred in. John and I had the honor of sponsoring them, which is always fun because the responsibilities include showing the new people around, helping them find a place to live, entertaining them and introducing their family to others in the squadron. They had two precious little girls, Stephanie and Stacey. I liked Blaster and Susan immediately. No stranger to sarcasm myself, their quick wits and dry

Flight Suit Party

senses of humor made for a fast friendship for us. It was also obvious that they had a very close relationship, as a couple and a family.

A favorite activity for the guys in the squadron was meeting at the 67th squadron bar on Friday afternoons right after work. They talked about the week and generally blew off steam. The wives were invited and several of us joined them, from time to time. The guys also went on temporary duty (TDY) regularly and would often be gone for weeks. Living in a foreign country like Japan made social activities with friends very important to everyone's sanity.

During one squadron TDY the wives decided to have what we called a Flight Suit Party. We all donned our husbands' flight suits, rolled up the sleeves and cuffed the hems, and met at the squadron on a Friday night. We did most of what the guys did when they meet, but a little more upscale. We brought our own hors d'oeuvres, popped popcorn, and drank a few adult beverages. Some of the wives played Crud, a game played by most Air Force pilots, loosely based on pool, but played on a Snooker table. Susan was there, as she was at most of the wives' activities. At a recent squadron reunion in Virginia we relived the fun we had those nights and laughed at the pictures of us in our husbands' oversized flight suits, and laughed even harder at our oversized, 1980s hair.

Stacey, Susan, me, and Stephanie, just before the accident.

PART THREE

ACCIDENTAL LESSONS

Roger Wilson and me at the YMCA.

CHAPTER NINE

EARLY RECOVERY AND MOVING BACK TO COLORADO

Getting released from the hospital and back to real life was like jumping out of a plane with no parachute. By the way, I've never done that. At first, it was dealing with the immediate challenges of physically moving me and addressing my everyday needs. I was unable to communicate normally. The words were in my head, but they did not come out.

I didn't start eating anything until sometime in April or May after the accident. I had to prove I could safely swallow in order to take food orally. Before that, I was fed liquids intravenously. Then I "ate" through my nose with a tube that went directly to my stomach. Finally, food was delivered through a gastrointestinal tube, which allowed larger amounts of food and liquid to enter directly to my stomach. I never thought I would actually enjoy being fed in this way, but it was better than starving. I had dropped fifty pounds to 135 pounds and being fed through the tube stabilized my weight. When I began eating on my own, the gastro tube was removed, and I started to regain some of the weight I had lost.

I now required constant supervision, and the people helping me had to make sure I did not hurt myself. It was also important that the people taking care of me did not hurt themselves in the process. I am not a small person and the simplest movements, for example moving from the bed to a chair, or a chair to the toilet, now were major strategic operations. Not to mention, I could not speak well, and that complicated things further.

My early speech therapies focused on memory and swallowing. Then I had to work on being understood. I knew exactly what I wanted to say, but could not communicate clearly. I had to practice the most basic sounds in order to improve my speech so

I could start to be understood. The speech therapists helped me work on sounds over and over again. They were very patient. I was not. It was frustrating and quite scary to have my thoughts trapped inside my head because the sounds coming out of me didn't make sense.

We had decided to return to Colorado Springs. There was a VA hospital nearby in Denver and a clinic in Colorado Springs. My medical needs would be met. Our family's livelihood and family support made Colorado Springs ideal. Though I was still on active duty when I was injured, Susan needed to do what she could to continue her military career and get support I couldn't provide. For work, not only is the Academy there, but also Peterson and Schreiver Air Force Bases. Perhaps most important in the early years, Susan had family forty-five miles south in Pueblo, and it was clear we were going to need all the support we could get.

For nearly a year I bounced between outpatient services at HealthSouth in Colorado Springs and three-week stints at the Denver VA, where I was released to spend weekends with Susan and the girls. It was always like being released from prison, not that I have any experience with prison. It was clearly not a normal situation, but it made me feel like life could be normal again.

For four years, we lived on Peterson AFB. Susan was able to transfer there, and we stayed in guest quarters until some red tape was cut and an on-base home had some modifications done to make it minimally accessible. Her parents and family would take turns coming up from Pueblo to be with me while she was at work and the girls were at school. Susan knew that getting me out of hospitals and assisted living situations was in my best interest. I needed to be with her and the girls. They had always been my heart. Now they were my lifeline.

Susan was working five days a week. Her parents would try to come as often as possible to watch over me, but they couldn't be there all the time. Many people didn't understand that I needed to be watched constantly during those early days in my recovery. I had to spend time in adult daycare for the disabled. The employees and other people were nice enough, but it's hard to create any care system like that, that meets the needs of everyone. I entered a program intended for people with TBI that were in transition to independent living. Unfortunately I was the only client in that category. My cohorts were generally elderly people transitioning from independent living. We were not on the same path and personally, I wanted a lot more help with physical therapy than the service was designed for or could provide.

Susan was persistent and fearless as she negotiated my situation. She had always been a strong woman, a key reason to her appeal. Now, she planned my recovery and return to living at home with military precision. She was a rock. And I pitied anyone who tried to tell her what to do, or what was best for me.

I had already heard many things I did not like and did not want to believe. Doctors at the VA in Minneapolis, and now at the Colorado Springs VA, told me I might never walk again. That was the first huge motivator. I was going to prove them wrong, and I didn't care how long it would take.

Physical therapy was now a huge part of my life. I was motivated because my goal was to walk again. I've always enjoyed working out, so this was not a change. It just required more determination. I used to work out when I was a fighter pilot in order to not lose consciousness while flying and pulling nine Gs. The military doctors told us fighter pilots to work out in order to keep our G tolerance high. We learned to stay conscious by working to keep blood from pooling in our extremities. So, I had some background in staying alert. I saw physical therapy as a natural extension of what I had already experienced in flying.

Physical therapy is incredibly demanding, harder than I ever would have guessed. Even with my history of physically demanding sports, my body was now challenged in completely different ways. And the only competition was myself. I really missed competing with others.

I met some amazing people during the early years back in Colorado Springs. Some were doctors, nurses and therapists. Others were new neighbors and others old friends from before the accident, who have hung in there with me on my new mission to walk.

Roger Wilson, my personal trainer, became my new wingman. He has probably been my luckiest find and biggest help since I returned from Minneapolis. I have worked with Roger a long time. When I first started rehab at HealthSouth, there was a speech therapist named Val, who introduced me to Roger's brother. My wife says when I talked to Roger's brother, who worked independently but in a step-up type rehabilitation program, all I wanted to talk about was walking. So he and Val gave me Roger's phone number, and I called him. Val and Roger were so kind and willing to try to help me start working toward my goals. When Roger and I first got together, he took me to lift weights and helped me to start walking with my arm around him at Peterson AFB gym. Poor guy.

In 2000, we moved to our new accessible house. Roger was gracious enough to continue working out with me. We started going to the YMCA, a mile and a quarter from our home. He never put me down and has always listened to what I have to say. I've learned a lot from Roger, and he has a say in all I do. He can always tell me what I did correctly and what I did incorrectly.

Roger has taught me a lot over the past fifteen years. For instance, if he tells me I'm not stepping far enough ahead or I'm leaning too far right, I listen and take what he says into consideration. Because he doesn't say much. If he says anything, you better listen.

I remember when I first got back to Colorado, Susan signed me up for outings with the City Parks and Recreation Group and the Breckenridge Outdoor Education Center. These were organized activities for disabled people, and it's safe to say I genuinely hated almost all the activities. I used to dread going on these outings, because I felt like all of us disabled humans were being put together for activities where we would have to have fun whether we would reach our potential, or not. Now, I feel much different about it, and look forward to wonderful times with great people.

The staff and volunteers are there to help participants have a good time and reach their individual goals, even if it's as simple as getting out of the house. No one is there just to criticize the participants like I did when I first participated. I was still too worried about been seen as disabled, so I didn't think I would ever have a good time on activities like this. I missed my favorite outdoor activities with my brothers and sister, but they lived far away, so, we couldn't go fishing or white-water rafting on the drop of a penny, or is that a hat?! I can't remember.

Now I don't think twice about taking advantage of any opportunity that might be available. I'm more comfortable with almost everything I do. And I've overcome much of my previous judgmental attitude toward people, because of how they look, sound, and what they say, or how they say it. I'm doing much better in Parks and Recreation activities. I can now walk, with help from the staff, from my wheelchair to the sit-ski whether on the snow or in the water. I am getting much better at water-skiing, or as I like to describe it, sitting on my butt, and not drowning!

I first went water-skiing with the Parks and Recreation Therapeutic Recreation Program at Prospect Lake, here in Colorado Springs. I tipped over the first time I got up, and then made it four times around the lake on my next try with the new "sit-down ski" they purchased specifically for my needs. I have no complaints, and I'm actually having a very good time.

As for snow-skiing, I go with an assistant who helps me down the runs and keeps me from losing all control! I've been hoisted up on rock-climbing walls, ridden a recumbent bike, and participated in competitions for disabled athletes. I've come a long way and I have a great time.

Staying active helps me meet new friends and prove to others that TBI is not going to keep me down. People have seen me involved over the years, and many folks tell me my speech and walking have improved. That's what really counts, when people who haven't seen me in a while tell me I am talking better, or walking more independently with their help.

Another friend I met when we moved to our neighborhood was Kendrick Sneckner, who went by Rick. I guess one day he reached out to help and seemed really interested in me as a person. He also had a lot of good ideas, like a grab bar in the bathroom, and special floor markings to remind me where to stand so I wouldn't go crashing to the floor. He was willing to stay with me or have me stay at his house when Susan had to be out of town. He would pick me up and we would go out to eat, and see a movie.

I can't say I've kept all my friends from before the accident, I think it's tough for some of them to connect with my changes, although some people have become even better friends. Many of my new friends have different kinds of personalities, and they don't know me from before, so don't have those experiences to compare. Most of my friends from my hometown in Milwaukee, though I don't see them much, remain good friends, and I can still talk to them, as always.

The location of our house was important, and it has definitely worked well. We are close to the YMCA, public transportation, stores and parks. Slowly, but surely, I learned to navigate bus schedules and getting to appointments and errands on my own. We are very close, within 1.5 miles to the YMCA, the bank, Target, and Safeway.

This is a great distance for my power chair. It can make that distance, twice—down and back up, and then again before it needs to be recharged. We can drive to the VA in Denver in an hour and a half, and it's even closer to get to the VA here in Colorado Springs. The local buses will take you just about anywhere, though sometimes those trips may be followed by a very long wheelchair ride. Springs Metro will take you anywhere you want to go as long as it is in the city.

People know me at the bank and the places I go frequently. Most are willing to help, and treat me like a person, not just someone in a chair. The people that go to

YMCA are especially kind, just like the management and the workers.

I've definitely become a more knowledgeable disabled person since getting here to Colorado in 1996. I still have my bad days, but the length between these bad days is certainly increasing! So, I just keep trying to overcome the negatives, accept the positives, and keep going.

OTHER PERSPECTIVES

Susan Hirst, *Wife*

Colorado welcomed us in late August. This time it was my parents who filled the gap in the day while the girls started school and I was back at work. Our transition included adult day care, outpatient rehab, and meeting our new friends and neighbors. Stephanie and Stacey adapted well to their school. Home, however, was a totally different challenge. What should have been the most carefree years of their young lives now required they feed their dad, help him in and out of bed and on and off the toilet. When Steve progressed to showering himself, one of the girls would sit just outside to listen for his calls for help and relay the need to me as I did my best to fix meals, wash clothes, or prepare for another day of school and work. When I was grocery shopping or away, the girls would "sit" with their dad. A particularly difficult discovery for me was when Stephanie had to "clean" Steve, not something an eleven-year-old girl should ever have to do for her father.

Fortunately, life got better and we settled into a new normal. Stephanie and Stacey were active through middle school and high school. They were members of the band, swimmers, club players of softball, soccer, and volleyball. Like many families, we were always on the road. Most every weekend, year-round, included a sporting event and though Steve could no longer coach, he could support. To this day we are recognized—could be the wheelchair! Hotels were a challenge in the 90s and early 2000s. We needed two beds and handicap accessibility, not easy to find and harder still to get anyone to understand the need. So, we paid nearly double what a family of four typically paid because we couldn't get our needs met in one room. On top of that the girls often were not even in a room near ours as adjoining rooms are few and far between. These girls grew up quickly. They were not even teenagers with their own hotel room, cell phones (when that wasn't the norm), and taking city buses to get to school and transfers to make it to sports practice.

The girls matured and their relationships with their dad changed. We all tried counseling. Stacey didn't talk, Stephanie who didn't want to talk, spilled out her frustrations, cried in anger and moved on. She didn't need more "talk therapy," but I think she benefited from the little she had.

Stephanie accepted Steve's changes and got mouthy and seemed to treat him like many teens treat their parents. Yet, she never was embarrassed or ashamed of him or his differences.

Stacey suffered greatly with Steve's TBI. He didn't recover to the man he was, and she lost not only her daddy, but also her buddy. Though she was loving, she was not happy. Her junior year in high school, eight years after the accident, she came to me saying she was unhappy, didn't like her dad, and didn't want to feel this way. She was ready to deal with the injustice of it all. A couple months of "talk therapy," and Stacey turned a corner. A bit of a changed young lady, Stacey began anew, not as reserved and ready to move forward boldly. The following year Stacey was captain of her soccer, softball and swimming teams, and senior class president. She headed to Seattle to college, far from friends and family, wearing a smile and set for adventure.

Stephanie Mitchell, *Daughter*

I don't know when it started, but my parents made sure we could participate in everything. It is almost as if my mom was so concerned that we would not be given opportunities, that she wouldn't let herself say no, regardless of how difficult or insane it made her schedule. I have to ask sometimes how she did it, but I never understand. One parent working full time, another parent who could not drive and needed care of his own, and two young daughters involved in every sport and activity possible and attending private school, there just aren't enough hours in the day. That shouldn't be mentioned without some special thanks to all those friends and their parents who cared about our family and helped us to make practices and games when our regular forms of transportation weren't possible. That normal transportation usually involved at least one leg on the city bus. The city bus led to some pretty great experiences, including one memorable meeting with Yahweh, a man in full robes and the stories to prove he was The One. I even think Stacey was asked out by more than one, too old to be appropriate, mentally handicapped men. A trip home from school during our 6th and 4th grade years that took no less than six hours because of a snow storm, and we didn't even have cell phones!

I think it was my sophomore year in high school; I was sitting high in the bleachers with a new girl at the school. We had known each other for a couple of weeks and were just hanging out while all of our friends played. My parents had come to the game as well. As everyone knows, my dad likes to walk whenever there's a rested (although that's not necessary) and willing person to help him. I'm pretty sure the lucky guy was our friend Gene that night; he was there to see his daughter play. As my dad made the long and unstable walk towards the bleachers the girl next to me said something like, "Ugh, gross. That weird drunk guy is staring at me." Obviously, she was new, because the school was not big and everyone knew us, it was an unfortunate position to be in for her. As the slow walk continued I didn't say anything, I probably said, "uh huh," in response to her comment. Then they started to climb the bleachers, right up to a row very close to ours. As they got ready to turn and sit down, while I'm sure my dad was still "staring" I smiled and said in a very cheerful voice, "Hey Dad!" The girl asked, "He's your dad?!" I turned to her with a smile and said, "Yes, he's my dad, and by the way, he's not drunk. He's got a brain injury and is in a wheelchair. I'm sure he was staring up here, but it was probably at me and wondering who I was with." I felt bad for her. I also told her you just never know and maybe it's not always about you. That definitely taught me a lesson as much as it did her.

Roger Wilson, *Personal Trainer and Friend*

I first met Steve in 1999, when I was working with my brother in vocational rehabilitation. A speech therapist friend of ours, Val, had met Steve, and wanted me to meet him and talk to him. He came to my office, which was super small, and I remember he couldn't even get his chair through the door. I knew he had been a fighter pilot and he was living at Peterson Air Force Base, and really wanted help with working out. Seeing this former fighter pilot trying to wedge his chair into my tiny office really made an impression on me. I still get choked up when I think about it

I quickly realized his new vocation was learning to walk again. We originally started meeting over at the base gym, and he was in pretty poor shape. He couldn't walk without the walker or leaning on me. But he was amazingly determined. And he never wanted anyone to feel bad for him—he just wanted to walk.

After he and his family moved off-base to their new home, I agreed to keep working with him at the local YMCA. He would motor down to the YMCA in his power chair and I would meet him there. Sometimes if the weather was bad, I'd give him a ride. Wheelchairs don't do so well in deep snow.

I started him on a weight regimen, then the exercise bike and the treadmill. Over time, he got stronger and eventually could walk with me around the entire gymnasium once, and sometimes twice.

We fell down once, as we were walking from the YMCA to the car. I was behind him, holding on to his belt, and his walker caught on the curb. He went down, and pulled me down right on top of him. But, he was fine, we got up, and somehow he managed to tease me about it.

Over the years, we've become very good friends. He knows my parents and I know his family. He's been through a lot, even ended up getting a knee replacement a few years ago, and we are working together to get him back to where he was before the surgery. He has fought through a lot of pain, before and after, but he never gives up. I've learned to understand his sense of humor. He never cuts me any slack, probably because he doesn't want me to cut him any. Once I twisted my ankle and he told me my injuries didn't count. When I complained about my carpal tunnel, he just gave me that look and said, "Oh you poor thing!" With a smile, of course.

Now I tease him right back. If the Air Force Academy has a bad basketball season, I kid him that he could play on that team. I think exercise and working out is tremendously important for him. It makes him mentally sharper. And it's good for me—it gives me enormous perspective and he has been an unexpected and excellent friend. And now he's on me about my losing some weight! I'm sure he'll get me into shape.

Kendrick Sneckner, *Neighbor and Friend*

I moved to Colorado Springs in 2000, just a block and a half from Steve. We met shortly thereafter at a neighborhood gathering, a wine-tasting group. Probably the second or third time we were together at a similar neighborhood gathering, Steve asked me to help him out in the restroom. Because of how it was configured he couldn't negotiate it by himself. That was the first time I stepped across the threshold of actively helping Steve out like that, which nobody really does in his life except for Susan, as far as I've seen anyway.

Traveling back and forth to Texas for my work at that time kept me coming and going a lot, but I started taking Steve out for eventful outings, from lunches to movies to running errands. There's a pretty neat story that happened when I was crippled for a short time with a cyst on a nerve in my lower back. It was so enlarged I was told it was probably cancerous, but it turned out to be benign. Regardless I could not walk, so I did not hesitate to have the inevitable talk about getting a chair for ME!

Before that happened, I had some treatments and steroids were injected into the cyst making everything worse for a time, though the pain could not get worse. It was horribly painful and debilitating. In the end the injection worked and the cyst shrank back from pressing on the nerve. I had made a vow to myself during my suffering that I would know I was on my way back when I was able to help Steve again. That opportunity presented itself the first day I was able to take my first steps again after the treatment, when Steve called and asked if I could take him to the Denver VA Hospital to get his new wheelchair.

I remember going in to my now ex-wife and saying I had to go to Denver, and her saying, "You can't go to Denver. You can't walk!" And I said yes I could walk and I tried to show her, but it wasn't very convincing and she said, "See, you can't walk." But I figured I could walk if I was pushing Steve because I could hold his chair when I was pushing it. And so, I wouldn't listen to her because I wanted so much to walk again, and I knew what it would mean for Steve to get his new chair. So, I used crutches to get to the car and went and picked up Steve. And just like I planned, when we got to the VA I was able to walk without crutches by pushing him in his old chair. To be perfectly honest, there were tears, and it was a lot harder than I thought because I was really weak . . . but we got his new chair.

Most of my time with Steve was getting him out: to eat, go to movies, watch a ball game, or do something interesting. We had a really wild ride at the golf course, when I was letting Steve drive the cart, once. We both survived it; that was the main thing. Another was meeting Steve in Corpus Christi, Texas, to take him fishing. We had a blast, but the real-world issues were a part of the trip.

He fell one night and called to no avail because I didn't hear him. I had to fix the downstairs bedroom so he could manage getting to the bathroom better. But the magic kicked in when we were fishing for red drum. Our guide was just about to put us right on top of a feeding school, which he did. But right before we started casting, a pod of porpoise showed up out of nowhere and started playing with the reds, by flipping them up into the air. They would go spiraling in circles and splash back in the water, right in front of us. It was quite an incredible thing to see. Then we started casting into the school and pulling out huge reds. There was no way for Steve to do any of it conventionally, so I was on my knees helping him hold the pole while he reeled in the fish. Humbling. It got to everybody on the boat, of course.

We've had a running comedy routine of trading barbs, and making fun of each other. I'm usually the butt-end of the jokes. But sometimes it really does get funny. I wish I had recordings of some of the exchanges they are so comical sometimes . . .

Dick Stadler, *High School Classmate and Friend*

Steve's accident and resulting condition hit me hard. It hit all of us. It was so difficult to understand why this had happened to him—I didn't even know how to think about it. Everything he had accomplished to that point was earned and deserved and authentic—it just seemed so wrong for him to be taken down at the top of his game.

When he was still hospitalized I remember contacting Coach Baer, and getting a high school jersey from him to take to Steve at the VA hospital. In the early years of his recovery, there was an event back in Whitefish Bay held at Cahill Park, where we spent so much of our youth playing basketball, skating and hanging out. We raised money for a fund to help him, and lots of friends and family showed up to see Steve, and offer what support we could.

He and Susan had moved back to Peterson Air Force Base, and he was really on my mind. I planned a trip out to Colorado to see him and see if I could help in any way. Looking back, it was almost selfish, as much for me as it was for him. Maybe I was searching for some perspective from my own concerns, minor in comparison to what he was dealt.

His girls were still young, and the family was still adjusting to some pretty tough new realities. I hoped I could give Susan a break and just spend some time with Steve. I was able to comprehend his new speech difficulties fairly easily—I understood what he was trying to say most of the time. He was having trouble holding his head up, and he desperately wanted to walk.

For some reason, I came up with an idea to devise a device to strap to his head that involved a beeper and a level, so that when his head drooped, the beeper would prompt him to pull his head up and get it level. We spent the better part of one day running around to various stores looking for all the parts to put it together. Of course, Steve was game, and wanted to try and walk everywhere we went.

He really couldn't do it, but we did it anyway. He is so big and solid, but he was still unstoppable—just new goals. I went with him to the girls' basketball games, to therapy sessions, to the store. His assets were challenged, but Steve still had them and has relied on them to this day.

When he comes back to the Milwaukee area to visit, we always try to go out and have dinner with friends. It has been a life road back, fueled by so many things: anger, depression, frustration, but also his astounding ability to persevere. The guy just does not give up.

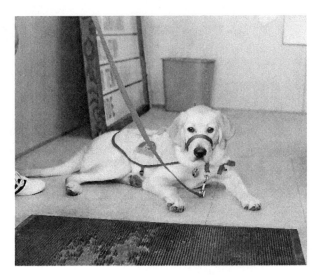

Nyla as a puppy.

CHAPTER TEN

MY GIRL NYLA

About six years after my accident, an attractive blonde came into my life. She had the most beautiful eyes and the most intelligent way of looking at me. Her name was Nyla.

Nyla was a service dog, from Canine Companions for Independence. She was two years old when I picked her up in 2001. This was a brand new experience for me as I never had a dog when I grew up or during my first years of marriage.

I was somewhat excited when Val, the speech therapist, gave my name to the canine companion group in California. I had no idea how Nyla would change my life.

Right from the start, she was a great companion to me. She was able to pick up silverware and dishes off the floor I may have dropped while eating or cleaning up. She would bring them to me and I could then take them and put them in the sink. I must have dropped a lot of food on the floor, because she was somewhat overweight the first couple years I had her. Come to think of it, so was I. I learned how to keep her fit and maintain her optimum weight.

Just having her with me was a comfort if we were the only ones on the sidewalks or streets. Half Golden Retriever and half Labrador, she was very nice looking. Not knowing much about dogs, she seemed very intelligent to me and everybody who met her confirmed my opinion. People seemed friendlier when I was with Nyla. Nobody can resist a beautiful and well-behaved dog.

She took a lot of my time, but I didn't mind. I loved our routine together as much as she did. I'd get up in the morning and then get her out of her kennel. After I was dressed and had breakfast, I'd take her to the garage and feed her and give her some water. When she was through, I took her for a walk, or we would go to the YMCA for my exercise.

I wheeled around everywhere with Nyla. And people would see her and forget about, me! Everybody talked with her, and was so interested in her. When I have a really good workout, it lasts about two hours, and she would wait patiently for me, enjoying all the attention from the YMCA workers and other members. Following my workout, we would go the bank, Target, and the Safeway, which are right across the street from the YMCA.

Nyla and I usually went to those three places. All the workers and most customers knew us, and it was nice to be known! I would joke that I was being ignored, because Nyla got so much attention.

This type of interaction took place everywhere I took Nyla. I didn't really ever want a dog but she trained me pretty well. She didn't mind that I was disabled, and I think she made it easier for people to strike up a conversation and greet me.

When we traveled, we hired a dog sitter. She was always happy and excited when we returned. Nyla loved going places with me and kept me company when I was writing at the computer or home alone.

Nyla had excellent manners. She never bit another animal or any person. I would have been required to give her back if she ever bit anyone. However, one day she was bitten by two German Shepherds near the YMCA!

As we walked by the baseball diamond, she was suddenly attacked by these two unleashed monsters while she was attached to my chair. I guess we were both easy targets, but they were more interested in Nyla. If she had not been attached to me, I could not have moved quickly enough to restrain her or intervene.

The man and woman owners barely reacted when their dogs attacked Nyla, and didn't even apologize, insisting she was fine. I was probably too shaken up to confront them and too scared to hang around. So, I started home, but as we were getting away from the YMCA, Nyla started bleeding pretty heavily from the bites on her back.

We turned around and went back to find the attackers, but they had taken their dogs and gone home, conveniently disappearing from the scene of the crime. Apparently, they were used to it. When I went back the next day to try and find them, a nice lady who was

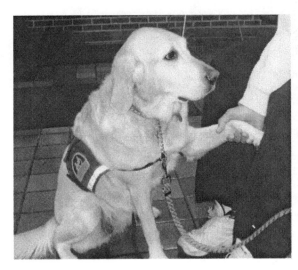

My best friend.

their neighbor told me that type of thing happened all the time.

I never did find the dog owners, but I hope they were caught by someone else. I actually felt sorrier for the dogs, having to live with humans who were so rude. We had to take Nyla to the vet and it cost $250 to get her stitched up and protected from infection.

By the time Nyla was about ten years old, she was starting to slow down a bit. The canine companion folks said it was getting time to retire her from active duty. She had been a loyal and hard-working companion, and she had earned the right to be a normal pet, and lie around and sleep all day if she wanted to.

They took her leash with them, but luckily, not her. She was still always by my side in her dog bed as I wrote my book or updated my journal.

But I really missed her being constantly with me as I went about my errands. The people in the neighborhood and various places we frequented had grown to love her and were disappointed not to see her with me. She always got a lot of attention and more than a few treats.

One day, I found her on the floor and I knew something was not right. I called Susan and she came home and rushed Nyla immediately to the vet. She was bleeding internally, and she died at the vet's office. I was devastated. She was truly a member of the family, and suddenly she was gone forever.

To this day, every time I leave a spot I am parked, I feel like Nyla will be in the way, so, I have to warn her "here I come, look out!" And she never is in the way, because she isn't even around. I miss her. She taught me a lot about unconditional love.

OTHER PERSPECTIVES

Stephanie Mitchell, *Daughter*

Nyla was most definitely the nicest one in the family. She may have been trained and given to my Dad but she was a great companion to us all. She was a great friend and maybe even a sort of therapist with her kind eyes—such an attentive and silent listener! I saw her shortly before she died and it was heartbreaking. It seems like she was retired just before she really started to show her age.

My mom told me the news when she died—it was upsetting. Now when I return home, every trip is a little sad when she isn't there to greet you or cuddle with you on the floor in front of the TV. My dad is resisting our attempts to convince him to get another companion dog. He thinks there is no way he can ever love another dog the same way. While I think he should get another companion, I think he is probably right. Nyla was truly a best friend and amazing soul.

Susan Hirst, *Wife*

Nyla was connected to Steve through Canine Companions for Independence. Nyla came from the Southwest Region in Oceanside CA, near San Diego. She was actually raised for her first year by a couple in Colorado Springs, John and Mary Litchlyter. CCI is a great organization that does so much good with service dogs and their "owners." John and Mary stayed in touch with us, and followed Nyla through her time with our family.

CCI can be found online at **cci.org.**

My motorized chair and Nyla, my public relations manager.

CHAPTER ELEVEN

MY CHAIR AND MY THRONE

I was determined to walk again but first I had to learn how to negotiate in a wheelchair and be able to take care of myself in the most basic ways. Some of my worst experiences involved getting in and out of the chair, and on and off the toilet, my throne. I tried to make light of it, but it really wasn't so fun.

We had moved back to Colorado Springs thinking that the proximity of the VA Hospital, the Air Force Academy and Susan's family would make a lot of the transition to living with a TBI much easier. And it has been a great place for us. But some of the most obvious things were not so easy.

People really treat you differently when you are in a chair. You become overly obvious or invisible, depending on the situation. A typical example is my famous parking lot experience. As I was moving from a local parking lot to take the handicap ramp to the sidewalk, there was a car driving immediately behind me that seemed to be in a hurry. I looked back and saw a man driving with a woman passenger in the front seat. Suddenly he sped up to get in front of me. Had I known he was going to go around me and do what he did next, I would have blocked his way and never let him get his car around me. He sped by me and pulled into the clearly marked handicap space between me and the handicap ramp!

The ramp is usually in between two disabled spots in a parking lot. I was livid! I wanted nothing more than to physically and verbally attack them, but I didn't, because he and the woman looked like they probably had at least one physical fight every month. And they looked like they never lost.

Speeding past me and blocking the ramp seemed almost planned. It was as if they had something against folks in wheelchairs. I don't know, but it sure felt personal to me. If I wasn't in a wheelchair and I saw this happen, I would have at least said something to the jerk. But I was feeling timid and there was no one around to help me.

When they got out of the car, they both just stood and looked at me. Then they smiled and walked past me into a completely different store!

When I thought about it later I wished I would have said or done something, and not let them get away with it. After this happened I felt like the lowest piece of scum on the face of this earth. Looking around the parking spot I saw many stores, but I couldn't cry to them and ask if they saw what the "jerk" did. I tried to think what I would do if it happened again. I knew not getting in a physical fight was the best plan. But I had to be careful about getting into a verbal fight, too, because smarting off could lead to a physical fight.

There are others who seem actually afraid of someone in a chair. In February of 2008, I scheduled a haircut at the mall and then went to have my fingernails and toenails cut. A guy with a wife who looks like mine has to keep himself looking good.

I got my haircut first. Then I went to get nails cut on my fingers and toes. When I first tried getting in the door, an older Asian man who might have been the owner and a female employee tried to block the doorway with their bodies. But I kept going and I could tell the pain they were suffering by the scared looks on their faces. They kept telling me I couldn't come in the shop.

I asked them several questions about why disabled people couldn't get their nails cut in their shop? They couldn't come up with very intelligent answers, but she finally agreed to cut my fingernails and toenails. When she cut one toenail, she also cut part of my toe which started to bleed and hurt. I could have kicked her in the face, I was so shocked. The owner had left, so he was not there to see where she cut me. I was so angry I refused to pay, so they were about as happy when I left as when I arrived. When I told my wife later and showed her my toe, she didn't believe me! She thought I cut my toe by myself.

Spending most of my time in a wheelchair means I am often at the mercy, good and bad, of other people. One day at Target, a guy cut in front of me and two other people who were in line checking out. It really brought this disabled man's temper way up. I could have said some bad things to that guy. Instead I calmly went up to him and said, "You just cut in front of three people." He just ignored me. He never even looked to see who was talking to him. I wanted to say some very personal things to really piss him off, but he didn't look like he would listen or care. Before my car accident, if I had seen this happen to somebody in a wheelchair, I would have backed up the guy in the wheelchair. And I would have definitely said something pointed and personal to the line-skipper if he didn't respond to the guy in the wheelchair. The part that upset me the most was being completely ignored, as if I didn't exist.

I don't think there are many people as rude and obnoxious as this guy in Target, but I had to say something to him. Otherwise he might just make it a habit. I was the only person who said anything about his wise-ass behavior. Incidents like this made me feel completely inferior, as though I had no right to be in front of this healthy guy who had decided that his business and time were more important than mine at Target. To be honest, it made me feel like crap.

Then I saw what happens when the good guys take action against the bad. Target roped off the area to make it impossible for people to skip to the front of the line. Target made things right for me very quickly. It showed me that if people are rude they will get what they deserve. I went to Target to thank them for roping off the line, and the guy told me Target Management came up with the idea. When you are in a wheelchair and at the mercy of other people, it feels great to see the good people step up and draw the line.

Another day, I was getting ready to cross the street when a man stopped his car right in the middle of the crosswalk. I kept motoring in my power chair like I was going to run into him. But, of course, I didn't. I didn't even call him a bad name. I really wanted to do both. Instead I drove my wheelchair around the back of his car as he waited for an opening so he could go on his merry, ignorant way.

This guy didn't even roll down his window and apologize. But he probably didn't even think he was wrong. Maybe I should have let him know with my middle finger. It is infuriating that people in their comfy cars don't even look at who they are endangering or blocking. Imagine if a youngster on a bike was on the same path!

Situations just like this have happened to me quite often over the years. I had been going to Safeway most weekdays for several years when I realized I had been taken advantage of. I knew someone was stealing from me. After finishing my workouts at the YMCA just across the street, I'd typically motor over to Safeway to have a sandwich made for my lunch, and pick up some of my favorites—Gatorade, Coke, cookies, apple fritters, or flavored milks (banana, vanilla, chocolate).

Sometimes in Safeway I had a helper to shop and pay, sometimes I would do it on my own, and other times I asked the cashier to help with my money. I didn't think this was a problem and as it turns out I trusted people when I shouldn't have. Over a period of time I felt I was missing money in my wallet. I tried thinking what I'd spent it on and came up with nothing; so, I started paying close attention to my habits.

One thing that stood out was a certain cashier who I used often. He would turn his back on me as he helped me make the right payment. I'd give him my wallet and have him take what was needed and return the change. He didn't always face me while doing this. I was suspicious so I set up a test. From the YMCA I went to the bank and asked the teller to count my money in my wallet. I then went to Safeway and did my normal routine. I chose the cashier I suspected of taking from me and, as usual, asked him to take the money from my wallet that was needed. I paid close attention and saw what he took from my wallet and after finishing my purchases I counted what was left. I don't remember all the details but I think twenty dollars was missing. Right then I went to the Customer Service desk and the clerk called the manager down. He counted my money and said they would review the tape. I never saw the cashier again. I think he was fired. I can't believe that there are people that would do this to me or anyone. I can only imagine what other disabled people go through. I'd been laughed at, ridiculed, and now stolen from. I now think that many people are bad. I don't like to feel this way but it just seems to be true.

Then there are the people who think you need a hand-out. I really don't want people thinking I'm a beggar, and giving me their loose change at a sporting event or other public place. I have never held a sign trying to explain my situation, but I have actually had people come up to me and try to give me money. I think I was in Milwaukee and it was after a Bucks game! I didn't say a word to him, not while he was giving me the money, or afterwards. It was a great event to witness. Those who were with me had something to joke about for a few weeks! I said we could have enough bar money if we could find a hat for me to hold out while I sat in my wheelchair, so people would get the idea!

On the other hand, there are truly kind people you meet when you are in a chair. One day I was on my way to the YMCA and my wheelchair started acting like it was running out of power. It was, because I forgot to charge it the night before. I thought I'd be fine because my power chair can make it down and back twice when it is warm outside, but it had been very cold. A gentleman stopped and pushed me home, which was about a quarter mile. The things nice people do for disabled people are truly amazing.

My walking continued to improve after I got my new titanium knee in May of 2009, but there were still times I would fall. In January 2010, Susan had left on a Sunday morning to visit Stacey in Baltimore. She had work in Washington, D.C. the remainder of the week until Wednesday. I was getting into my manual chair after taking Nyla for a walk. When I shifted weight from both legs to my right leg I fell down hard and I felt my tailbone go numb when I fell on it. But I knew I was not hurt. I lay on the garage floor estimating my chances of getting back in my wheelchair and getting the garage door open so someone could hear me calling for help, or see me crawling on the floor. I stood up with the wall helping me. I finally opened the garage door but I couldn't get back into the wheelchair. I yelled for help, and our neighbors next door and our neighbor from down the street helped me get back in my manual chair. But Nyla got out and she was lost for a while.

Later that day, Nyla slept on her cushion and I kept thinking about my fall. How the heck could I fall doing something I had done so many times with no problem before my surgery?! It bugged me, but I concluded I would just have to learn how to do it with a titanium knee.

My mother and oldest brother were visiting around the same time. And, just to make everybody comfortable, I fell once in the bathroom trying to transfer from the toilet to my wheelchair by myself as usual. Again, I wasn't hurt, but it bothered me. It was a demoralizing factor in my recovery because it seemed like I was getting worse.

Another time I was taking Nyla for a walk after she ate. I was taking her through the new part of a neighborhood with new houses and new sidewalks. Somehow, I came off the sidewalk and into a garden where I fell into a soft bed of wood chips. So, I just laid there and yelled for help. Luckily, a woman driving by heard me and stopped her car to help. I was way too big for her, so she called for help. The fire department came, got me into my wheelchair, and followed me home. Never a dull moment in this recovery!

My trips to the bathroom were often quite eventful and surprising. I never knew when my right knee would collapse and I would fall to the ground. One time I called Dr. Shea's office and left a message with his nurse Kim that my right knee gave out and I fell again in the bathroom! I was constantly thinking about falling in the bathroom, and I was constantly falling.

I didn't call an ambulance, but once I called our neighbor, and he came over to help me. I'd been getting up in the morning and going to the bathroom. I was tipping and falling to the floor, butt first. I had also been falling in between the wall and the toilet on the left side when you face the toilet. My back and right elbow looked very bad. I was getting up on my own somehow after the first time I called 911. Susan said I better not call 911 again unless I have a serious injury, or she'd give me one, sure she would.

I didn't call emergency, but I called Directory Assistance, and they connected me to our neighbor. He was over in a second, and he helped me to the wheelchair by moving it closer to the door and I got in my chair. Directory Assistance got to know me pretty well.

OTHER PERSPECTIVES

Susan Hirst, *Wife*

Sometimes I really hate that chair.

I want a husband who can hold me with two arms again, one that can run with me on a crisp fall morning, like we used to. I want a husband that takes care of me when I'm tired or one who fixes a romantic dinner when I get home from work. Maybe I've watched too much fantasy television, but it would be nice to go out on the spur of the moment and not have to make sure the choice of destinations has disabled accommodations. I want to sleep an entire night. I want to make it through one day where I don't see a wheelchair or have to help someone get dressed or eat.

Steve was, I now realize, the ideal. Until his accident, I had never changed a vacuum cleaner bag, and I can count on one hand the number of times I cleaned toilets, I did very little, if any laundry, and at least three days a week, dinner at home was not prepared by me. Suddenly, all these things belonged to me in addition to hanging doors, fixing stopped-up toilets, mowing the lawn, buying insurance, and dealing with sales people.

Time for a pity party?! More than sixteen years post-TBI, I regularly host just such a private event. There are not often guests other than myself, but occasionally a question and moment of honesty with a friend or an observation of something lacking in my relationship. I shed some tears, feel real grief, and scream inside at the unfairness of MY life. This is an indulgence I allow MYSELF, then I move on. It does little concrete good. Still I don't think it's such a bad thing. My feelings get out, I console myself, then I get on with it. Life is good, I am blessed, I have my husband and we live.

Bobby Renaud, *Air Force Academy Friend and Pilot*

After Arizona, I had gone off to fly the A-10 and Steve went on to the F-15. We sort of lost each other for a while. In fact, I had no idea he had been in a car accident until I heard the news and called Susan. I visited him at the VA in Minneapolis. It shook me to the core.

After they returned to Colorado, I called Susan and asked if it would be OK to come and get him for a weekend. I was flying for UPS, and I could jump-seat anywhere, anytime for free. So I flew out to Colorado Springs and picked him up, having no idea what to expect. Call me impulsive, I'll answer. It was Thunder Over Louisville the official start of the Kentucky Derby Festival, two weeks of parties and events leading up to the greatest two minutes in sports. Steve was having issues with his speech, but for some reason, I didn't have any problem understanding him. He was also having challenges getting around, and he just wanted to walk so badly. So even though he couldn't, he tried anyway, and I became the human mobile support system.

He stayed at our house, and I remember my kids just adored him. We went to my daughter Cherie's "Father-Daughter" dance and the three of us "danced" the night away. At home, we would get him out of his chair onto the living room floor, and Cherie and Philip would jump on him and have these massive tickle fights. We went downtown for the fireworks but the crowds made it difficult to maneuver with the wheelchair. It was hard to see him in this new reality, but he still knew how to have a great time, and his signature smile was still there.

Stacey Hirst, *Daughter*

I hate my dad's wheelchair. I hate it because for him, it is the most significant distraction to life. Walking has been his primary focus in recovery. It is as if by walking, he will heal all the hurt of his TBI. His wheelchair makes him angry. It makes me angry.

I cannot imagine what it must be like to be my father, a man who once had everything. The man that was my hero and my best friend, handsome, successful in every sense of the word, suddenly changed forever. I don't know what it is like to be inside his mind, inside his body looking out on a world that is so familiar, yet so different. I have spent much of my life hurting for him, hurting for my family, hurting for me.

But there is little reason for me to still hurt. There has been much suffering in my life, challenging experiences that have both been chosen and ones that have chosen me. My dad's TBI is a reality that cannot be changed. As my mom has always said, "Things don't happen for a reason, but you can make reason out of everything that happens." It has taken a long time to start living these words, to really believe them and believe in them. Sure, there have been times in my life when I have sought answers, sought reason for why my dad had a TBI. But it is useless time spent. There is no reason, there is no force that I can imagine that decided he should suffer in this way. It just happened. It's done.

Still skiing!

My Demons and My Angels

When I broke my wrist during that basketball game in high school, I took the injury badly. I had always been impatient, but my quiet nature had kept it in check. For the first time in my life, I saw things slipping away from my control. I knew I needed to play to keep the recruiters interested. Now, something completely beyond my control had sidelined me and prevented me from showing what I could offer a college team. I had gone from being a young man who had risen to meet every challenge, and who had gotten used to the idea that opportunities presented themselves to those who worked hard, to watching helplessly as a relatively minor injury derailed my future. I look back now and realize how little I knew.

At the time, it was the lowest point in my life. It was too early to remove the cast. It would be at least two more weeks before I could play again. Hearing those words from the doctor was like he had taken a hammer and shattered the bones all over again. I completely lost it and before I knew it, I was yelling at him, venting my pent-up frustration by questioning his medical knowledge and qualifications. I couldn't sit out another game, I screamed at him. I had to help the team. I had to keep the scouts interested.

Those broken bones may as well have been the shattered remains of my world. No basketball. No scouts. No scholarship. Nothing.

I knew then I had a temper. I was not proud of my reaction. I never wanted to lose control like that again.

Years later, in the hospital after the accident, I was visited again by the demons of anger. But this time, they moved in for a much longer stay. They brought a few friends: anger and impatience, depression and guilt.

The anger and depression that resulted from the TBI were new and unwelcome aspects of my post-accident personality. They have had horrible influences in my relationships, especially those most dear to me. I have not been easy to live with.

Stephanie and Stacey did not understand. They were still young girls, and they knew me as a much different person. Who was this angry man in the chair who looked like their dad? Why was he yelling?

I needed to treat them better. I really HAD to treat them better. Man oh man; it was a constant battle that eventually wore me down. Even when they were at college, we would fight on the phone or via e-mail. I never really saw the reason to be fighting, but when they see it, or said they saw it, I was constantly walking on egg shells.

I was not acting very well when coming out of my coma from what other people say. Nobody, not my mother, my wife, or anybody else says I was acting well. The scary thing is, I don't remember most of the horrible things I said.

I now make it a priority to treat people well all the time, unless they treat me badly. I may get seriously hurt one day, because of my reactions to the way bad people act.

This probably remains my toughest task, but I keep working to fulfill it. I'm really trying very hard to not get angry at people around me for no apparent reason. I usually react terribly when I'm angry, but I'm getting angry less and less. I try more to let it go, what was said, or whatever happened.

I've had quite a few family members tell me they hate me. My wife and both of my daughters have told me straight out that they "hate" me on more than one occasion. I've even had a few people in my original family tell me the same thing in so many words, although they didn't come right out and say "hate."

This hatred is probably brought on by things I say and do, but I just wish they would not say they hate me. I wish they would just tell me what is bothering them. It's very important to bring it out by telling me why they hate me, not just that they hate me. I hope they temporarily hate me, because they would never hate me forever! My friends don't say they hate me. But, as my family points out, my friends don't have to live with me forever, and they do. I'll keep trying to make things better.

All in all, Susan has done more than just what it takes to keep us all together, despite what she wanted out of life. We've suffered through some tough times. My TBI is very terrible, and the things Susan has done have kept the entire family together. We're not the same loving family we were before I crashed, but we still love each other.

We've learned a lot through the bad times. We've actually done pretty well in that category and we keep getting, better. My brain got so messed up in the crash a lot of bad things which happened family-wise were my fault. I know it sounds like I'm making excuses, but I'm not just blaming it all on the accident. The family relationships are what count and mean the utmost to me. Sometimes I missed or forgot what was happening in the most important parts of my daughters' lives. When the conversation leads to an important part of anybody's life I try to remember what happened. The stories other people tell me that I don't remember are the ones I try to memorize now, so at least it looks like I remember some of the things I forgot.

Marriage is hard work, and TBI doesn't make it any easier. There have been times my wife told me she was filing for divorce so I should get ready. I didn't believe her, but there are times I think she really meant it. I've called her very bad names at times, and she has called me names too, but not even close to the bad names I've called her. The ones I called her are much worse.

Susan met me at the VA and we told the counselor Louise Hisey what was going on between me and Susan. I'm not sure if those meetings ever helped, but I think over time, things got better.

Depression

I've had some periods of very dark moods. I'm feeling better now, but I was very depressed for a while. Deep down within, depressed.

I didn't know why. I really thought there was no reason to keep this sorry life going, on and on. But I knew I couldn't keep that "not living junk" going, because taking my own life would interrupt that of my daughters and others. I had to keep acting like life was super great.

Before the car crash everything in my family's life was great, so I desperately wanted to somehow get that way of life back. Every morning I know I cannot, and don't want to, act depressed. Because, bottom line, my life is a lot different than it used to be, but it still isn't too bad.

I think this injury has caused much heartache in me and my family and with our extended families. I know things I have done and said have caused a lot of depression for them. They don't see me the same way they did. Susan will tell me she doesn't lie to our children, especially when they ask her how she and I are getting along. She tells everybody the truth, including me. And fortunately, our children are the same.

At times, it has been harder to get along with the people closest to me. I wanted so much to get over it and become a loving family again. I've seen the start of it, and I want this more than anything.

I want to point out one thing: while suffering through this terrible car accident and the follow-on results I'm actually doing pretty fine physically and mentally. Going to the YMCA and working on things my physical therapists have told me has helped me in a lot of different ways and has encouraged me greatly, physically and mentally.

As I recovered from my knee surgery a few years ago, it was time to start walking again with Roger and finish off my workouts by doing something else, maybe sit-ups, and back exercises. My brain seemed to react favorably to doing something new and beneficial. This was a tough thing to do!

Pain

Pain really screws up your thinking, and it doesn't make TBI much better. I've included some journal entries that might give you an idea of what I'm trying to describe.

Tuesday, January 6, 2009

I was getting in bed Tuesday night and I was icing my neck and knee and when I was putting the ice in the container on my neck and it starting feeling like it was being stretched out of my body, and it felt like the pain wouldn't ever stop. So, I called Susan in Pueblo where she was visiting her parents. She offered to come home. And I said no way. And it was about midnight. So, after I hung up with her I called 911.

While the ambulance was coming, I got out of bed and waited for them at the front door. They took me to the emergency room of Penrose Main Hospital and I was checked out for about four hours. They gave me some shots in my neck and took blood from my forearms. And they gave me drugs for my neck and arms. But they couldn't give me drugs for the following days. They couldn't tell me how to get the drugs with my insurance, so, I said the Peterson AFB Pharmacy could get them and I would just have to wait.

Talk about terrible pain. I'm very glad that four hours of pain is over. When I was there they gave me some pain relieving shots which really helped. So, whatever they did really helped.

Saturday, January 10, 2009

Today started off pretty good. But my wife gets very angry with me when I don't read the labels on my pills correctly (I'm sure I read them correctly, but I don't under-

stand what they mean all of the time). Of course she's scared about it. She says "What do I have to do, write the directions down on paper?!" She was nervously shaking and not talking clearly and stuttering while she spoke, so, she was quite upset, because what I was saying was obviously senseless. But she said she'll still take me to the shopping mall to work with Nyla, because she doesn't want to hear me whine if I fail, or if they say I or someone needs to take charge.

Sunday, January 11, 2009

I'm very tired; I'm going to take a nap, now.

That was the "BEST" nap I've ever had! My neck was very sore when I got up, but didn't tighten up like usual and Susan graciously gave me the pills I was supposed to take at that time of day. So, my neck is sore, but I don't have the tightening like I had when I called the ambulance. I'm kind of scared for tomorrow morning, but Susan will put out the pills I need in a pile on the sink. So, I'm going in to tomorrow with a very positive attitude.

Friday, January 23, 2009

Here's something new: I went to the YMCA today and had a leg day, and I really had a good day lifting weights for my legs. I went without painkillers for the entire night. However, when I awoke I took one pain killer when I got up, because my right knee and leg were kind of hurting. I put Flexeril (stops my neck from continuously shaking) in my wallet where I have a zipper pocket, and it disappeared, unfortunately. I've just got to do what the doctor says to do. That turns out to be difficult, sometimes. I took a pain pill when I got home, because I was starting to get pain after I worked out at the YMCA.

I went to Safeway on my way home and got some lunch. I was very hungry since I had only eaten breakfast and it was four o'clock in the afternoon. When I got home Susan wasn't home. She was still at work at 6 p.m. on a Friday night. To be honest, that is part her fault, part the job's fault. When I was a fighter pilot it would be totally all the other fighter pilots' fault at the bar where we would go to unwind after a hard week's work.

I honestly wish I had any job now. But relaxing and going to the YMCA consistently is a great set-up now for my effort to get better in all those areas I suffered injuries. I would work my hardest at any job now, knowing what my choices are after getting *a Traumatic Brain Injury. I guess you can understand why I am writing a book after this mess. It keeps me very busy and from feeling sorry for myself. I'm over self-pity, anyhow. It all really hits home, so to speak, when you get a TBI. Nothing (physically or brain-wise) has been easy, ever since I came out of my coma, and started remembering things.*

Medical Care and The Veterans Administration

Dr. Tockish from the AFA Hospital found three tears in my right knee cartilage about seven or eight years after I returned to Colorado Springs. These were the first times I saw him, instead of the doctors at the VA. I was accustomed to hearing things like "Oh, come on there's no pain." People at the VA actually told me things like that when I continued to report my pain.

Dr. Tockish confirmed the tears in my knees with MRIs. I asked the VA about this. and they said they would have one of their doctors take a look at it, but the appointment never came. This was eight years after my car accident.

We were getting frustrated with the bureaucracy, so my wife decided to go elsewhere. Coach Popovich even offered to fly me down to San Antonio and have their team orthopedic take a look. By the time everything came together, Dr. Tockish had been transferred somewhere else, so the surgery was done at Penrose Saint Francis Hospital by Dr. McBratney, also from the Air Force Academy. She said, "Yes I'll take a look, put in a fake knee if required, and give you the results of the surgery."

I think the VA seems to only work with mind problems and they leave the physical things alone! I think the cost is the overriding factor. I complained about my right knee for about a year and they did nothing about it. We finally got a doctor at the Academy, one of the greatest orthopedic docs the Air Force has, and I got a fake knee implanted.

It seemed impossible for the VA to take the correct action when the pain, tears and arthritis were present.

My Angels

As I sit here thinking about my recovery I just can't help but think things are getting better! I'm no therapist, but some of the things I now can do, I would never have come close to a while ago. With all these demons of pain, anger, depression and guilt, I've been extremely fortunate that I've got combat troops on the other side, my angels. My family, friends and caregivers have stayed with me though the worst parts of my recovery.

Some angels have literally been invisible. We have not always known some of the people who have come forward with assistance and support. The generosity of those who have given with no need for thanks or repayment, has been humbling.

My everyday angels keep me in line. Susan, my daughters and my mother, are definitely the Head Angels. Without them, I would be very alone in this world. They have never given up on me, even when I'm sure I've pushed them away with my rage and anger. We've all grown up together since my accident.

My pilot buddies still have my wing. Some have flown me around, some have spent the gift of time with me and many have given me back memories through the stories they have contributed to this book.

On the Canine Companions for Independence website (www.cci.org) there is a sentence, "Some angels have wings, others have tails." I never would have had a dog, and then Nyla came along. She taught me and others a lot. Now she is a dog angel.

I'm told by many people I am an inspiration to them. Sometimes, I'm rolling down the street and someone comes up to me and starts talking to me and saying how inspirational I am to her or him, and others. That usually happens at least once per week. Now, this makes me feel great! I have a lot that keeps me happy.

A MEDICAL PERSPECTIVE

Dr. Bob Ireland, *Surgeon Specialist and Friend*

This is really the tough part about TBI. Steve's often continuous high G roller coaster of complex affects (anger, depression, pain, and at times, guilt) interacting with significant bodily challenges interacting with medications interacting with multiple levels and sources of medical care, and also interacting with profound and complex family challenges, are difficult to convey and understand. The levels of real and perceived chaos that have been experienced, and at some levels still persist, are perhaps the most devastating for persons with TBI and their loved ones.

Without the actual medical records to make sense out of why care was less aggressive in one setting versus another leaves a bit of a void inviting speculation that can certainly wax quite negatively for institutions missing diagnoses and not providing definitive care. Consideration of such in Steve's experience has larger implication as an underlying sub-theme for others with TBI. Our nation now is finally facing the fact that we are unprepared to deal with the number and severity of head injuries incurred by service members in current conflicts. More importantly, any impression that those who incur significant brain injuries can simply be "patched up" and sent home to continue their lives with their families must be dispelled, along with any notion that fails to address the extensive types and amount of resources that will be required for meaningful and sustained support for both the injured members, and the families who are injured in a significant way, as well.

OTHER PERSPECTIVES

Susan Hirst, Wife

I struggle. Supporting Steve is my first priority but it is challenging. He seems to have a complaint or demand every second. Pretty much from the minute I return from work until he has a diversion (phone call, visitor, etc.) he is either asking me to do something for him or complaining about what I haven't or what others have done. A greeting at the end of the day that includes "how was your day?" would throw me for a loop. I'm accustomed to be called to with urgency the moment Steve hears me enter the house. Instead of a typical greeting, I get something on the order of "I need . . . ," "you didn't . . . ," or "did you . . . ?!" My less than gracious response only escalates the situation. I suppose I should be pleased when my shortcomings aren't the focus, but I tire of the other complaints as well. Steve is quite positive in public but seems to save his frustrations for his one-and-only. If I didn't know better I'd think he was paranoid. Almost daily I hear about someone who talked down to him, laughed at his expense, blocked his way on the sidewalk, cut him off in the checkout line, hung up on him when he made a call, and on, and on. The same behaviors we all experience seem more egregious to Steve, or more directed because he's disabled rather than because the person has poor social skills or is just plain rude.

Whether it's someone parking in the reserved handicap space, blocking a curb cut-out, stepping in front of him because he doesn't move at their pace, talking around him, I don't think he has the filter in place to respond in the manner I think appropriate. Instead, he "over-reacts" and in doing so gives fodder to those who think the disabled are inherently mentally unstable. His response to these slights and down-right insults is aggressive. He charges toward and/or physically contorts against the offender, hollers out against the indiscretion, and generally embarrasses me with his reaction. I don't have a solution, and in the moment there is really no satisfaction in my words or interference. We can discuss a situation rationally and calmly when it's in the past. I wish I were patient enough to wait and let things ride.

Since our daughters have grown and moved away, what I do instead of handling the complaints, aggressions and slights, is to remove myself from the situation as much as I think reasonable. Steve and I spend a good amount of weekend time together, but during the week I am heavily involved in outside activities. My job has me out of the house Monday through Friday for eleven-plus hour days, including the commute. Add to that early morning workouts each day, pottery or another art class once per week, two evening book clubs per month, Bunco one evening per month, volunteer commitments two evenings per month, a giving circle once per month and as many other "social" activities as there are invites. To be "fair," I made a resolution to protect one evening each week to spend time with Steve. I haven't always been true to my resolution as I run from the challenge rather than explode from the pressure. I forgive myself for being selfish in this way but the guilt I feel when others comment on just how busy I am proves to me I have a lot to work on instead of running from.

(OK family and friends, you are welcome to skip this next brief note . . . thanks!)

I don't know if my brother-in-law remembers, but sitting alongside Steve's bed in ICU I asked out loud, to no one in particular, "What if I never have sex again?" Steve was still in a deep coma, I was imagining the implications of our lives, and this was a concern?! Interesting. Suffice it to say, some weeks or months later he passed a quick exam. Since then, ability is not the issue and the challenges are mine. I imagine that in a general sense we're not unlike many marriages.

For those who've wondered but haven't asked, Steve is perfectly willing and able. I on the other hand am not so eager. Whether it is the change in personality, the caregiver role, exhaustion, or the actual mechanics, this is an area I could certainly be more generous. Regardless of my "desire," this powerful and simple gift is completely within my control. The payback is obvious, yet again, it is a personal struggle.

Hate, divorce . . . yes, I've said those things. I've meant them, at least in the heat of the moment. I'm not seeking understanding. I just don't want to hold myself to too high of a standard. I'm not as strong as I may seem. Few people get to see my vulnerabilities because I'm afraid that by exposing them I won't be able to put them back in their place. Without that power, I'm lost. Living with someone you love who suffers from TBI can be a nightmare. Being told by others how great you are can be even more difficult, the pressure to be "perfect," do the right thing and behave in the right way is almost overwhelming. The challenges are never-ending. Sure, Steve is the same man inside. He has the same beliefs and values, his idiosyncrasies haven't changed; but Steve is completely different. His sense of humor, social filters, and language have all changed fundamentally. Unable to live the life he once had, he struggles to deal with the resulting frustrations. I'm his target. I struggle. I strike back. I'm ashamed.

Giving advice is so much easier for me than taking and applying it. "Can I help?" "Is there anything I can do?" "What do you need?" Picking up on those offers and accepting the goodness of others is difficult. I certainly don't want to burden anyone or show I'm unable to handle my life, so, I answer in the negative. It's a quick response, mostly inaccurate, but I don't know how to ask for or accept help from friends. If family asks, I have answers and can talk through ideas.

I don't want to put others out. I'm not looking for a lot and know that I don't ask for the little I wish was offered, perhaps if I asked. I rationalize that if they don't offer, they don't want to be asked, not necessarily an accurate assumption.

Don't get me wrong, we are not isolated from friends and family, several who have given wholly of themselves. Movies, lunches, dinners, Steve gets invites and he goes. He has even had a couple camping trips, neither of which were smooth sailing for the generous souls that made it happen, and several weekend getaways of which I was not a part including trips to Las Vegas, Colorado Rockies, Opening Day, deep sea fishing, fighter pilot reunions, adaptive ski trips and more. Those events make Steve feel much more complete than any trip or outing I make happen and there are plenty of those. Without me along, he gets to be just one of the guys. He's happy and it shows. The anticipation he experiences is such a gift.

The advice I give to others in my situation is to be ready to accept offers. Think of things you actually would like help with. Give the person who offers the gift of being able to assist. I have much to learn about using my own advice, but, I am learning. If you are the one offering assistance, think about concrete things you could do. I have offered, and been accepted, on hosting a loved one on an outing I plan and at my home amongst other friends. I've also "sat" with a family member so that the rest could get away for a few hours and not be uneasy about having a little break. I can do more and need to do so. Steve wants to help others and what better way for him to give.

A MEDICAL PERSPECTIVE

Dr. Bob Ireland, *Surgeon Specialist and Friend*

Susan describes a repeating pattern of Steve's behaviors upon her usual return home after absences at work and other activities. These patterns include demanding immediate assistance or complaints about what she has not done or complaints about what others have done. Such patterns tend to preclude empathic inquiries from Steve regarding how her life is going, and can be the opposite of Steve's more public positive persona. While such behaviors regularly occur in many couples without brain injuries or psychopathology and challenge their relationship, Steve's behaviors clearly appear related to his neurological injuries.

Indeed, frontal and pre-frontal cortical trauma involves those areas of the brain that mediate: empathy; irritability and aggression; and perseveration. Empathy requires working memory and other frontal functions such as recognizing cues of emotion in others. Irritability and aggression can be inhibited by normal frontal functioning, not as much after prefrontal injury. In addition, behaviors Susan observes upon returning home may be a form of perseveration, whereby similar complaints manifest over and over, irrespective of current context and situation.

A plausible explanation for Steve's usually more positive public behavior is he may be experiencing anxiety around those who do not know him well, compounded by his challenges reading their emotional states (low empathy). Such can readily lead to paranoia resulting in an irrational fear of others' intents and suspiciousness of their behaviors, triggering aggressive thoughts toward them. However, fear and anxiety can inhibit acting on such thoughts. When sharing at the end of the day his angry thoughts about those who may have mistreated him, Steve then allows his irritability toward others to show in the safety and comfort of his relationship with Susan.

Susan's survival strategy involving daily early exercise, employment and volunteer work, art classes, book clubs, various social activities, and Bunco nights appears to be working in combination with a dedicated weekday evening with Steve once a week, plus weekends. Finding the right tension between her commitments to herself for her own survival, and to Steve as her first priority, will likely be based upon the degree of his continued, yet now slow, recovery, and Susan's evolving sense of self and callings.

Our family at Stephanie's wedding to Pat Mitchell.

PART FOUR

LIFE LESSONS

Still climbing!

CHAPTER THIRTEEN

LEARNING TO BE ME

Hopefully we all keep learning things our entire lives. In some odd ways, TBI has taught me more than I ever would have expected. Before I was hurt, I had some of the best teachers and coaches anywhere. I never knew that this injury would provide graduate training in the truly important things in life.

Studying and hard work on my part were required, but the most amazing lessons have come through other people. Some people were with me before TBI, but have remained with me and adjusted and changed to support me along the way. Others I never knew that well or would never have met, and they have also changed my life. I certainly don't think I ever would have written a book. These are the accidental life lessons.

Faith

My mother has an unwavering faith in God, and she raised me to believe in miracles. I don't think she ever thought I would become one through TBI. She has been there like a vigilant angel through my entire life, first as a caring mom, and then as a lifeline through my accident and subsequent recovery.

When I question why this happened, she gently reminds me God has reasons. I am convinced miracles don't just happen. I think you have to pray, but also try as hard as you can to get yourself halfway to them.

Susan and I still go to Mass and participate in our parish activities. The girls went to a Catholic grade school. Those communities have been there for us.

TBI has made me question God and my faith along the way. If I keep asking for answers, perhaps I'll find a few. I'll leave the miracles to God.

Strength

My wife Susan is the strongest person I know, both physically and mentally. Before I was hurt, she was a competitor in the TV show, *American Gladiator*. She represented the Air Force, and was on two episodes. I surprised her during the taping of the second show and I think I gave her a little extra support. Not many guys can say their wife was an American Gladiator!

She was an intercollegiate swimmer for the Academy. She runs marathons, does triathalons and crossfit, and she can stand up to my solid mass. I could not have made it, physically or mentally, without her help.

She is strong emotionally as well. I am so proud of her. Not only has she raised two beautiful daughters, she's raised me. She has been a wonderful mother, a loyal and loving wife, a successful officer and civilian career woman, and a friend to so many.

I'm not saying she has never cried or been overwhelmed. We both have. We've had some epic "disagreements." But she has stayed with me, even when I know she would just as soon hop a one-way flight to a desert island with a bunch of books and a smooth Cabernet.

Focus

Having a focus or a goal makes a difference. When things get overwhelming, being able to focus on something puts everything in perspective. My daughter Stephanie has the most amazing ability to focus and to achieve goals. She decided she wanted to attend the Academy, and she did. She decided to compete in a triathalon, and she

Me and my mom.

did. She fell in love with a really nice guy and wanted to marry him, and she did. She has always had the ability to set a goal, focus on it, and achieve it. I've never seen her nervous or distracted for anything: sports, academics, or even trying to get into the Academy.

She ran in the Military Triathlon Championships in California, and placed third overall. Because of that she gets to represent the US Military in international competition. I think that was OUTSTANDING. I'm sorry I didn't get to go watch. She has worked hard, and she is phenomenal in all three events in a triathlon. Her running and running style are super, she bikes very well, and was on the swim team at the Academy.

Living with TBI requires focus. Sometimes it's making a meal in the microwave when I'm hungry. I write down my exercise goals so I can focus on my work-outs at the YMCA. By focusing on my writing, I can sometimes remember things I thought I had forgotten.

Compared to my previous life, these things may seem simple. But if I didn't set goals, I might start focusing on negative things. I strive to focus on the positive things in life. I will never stop focusing on my goals of walking and talking. My daughter Stephanie inspires me to stay focused.

Compassion

Even as a little girl, my daughter Stacey was unusually caring and patient for someone her age. Having a father in a wheelchair is no fun, especially during those years when you are somehow embarrassed by your parents no matter who they are. She didn't like the fact that I was disabled, but she took it all in and learned a lot.

One early challenge for her was taking the same bus to school that I had to take to get around town to my appointments. I was in the back and she was in the front with her friends. I think that was really hard for her, and I know she struggled with how the accident changed me so much.

She is also a great athlete and a leader. She thinks and feels things harder than other people. I believe her spirit and her thoughtful approach to the difficult things in life have made her a natural leader. She is also an amazing writer. She has a blog and writes about her experiences.

Now she works with developmentally disabled people in group home situations. These places are not always in the best neighborhoods, and the pay is about as close to volunteer work as it gets. But she is so good at this work, so patient, and she really cares about the residents as people. Just as she treats her dad, Stacey lives the word compassion every day.

Friendship

I've learned a lot of new things about friendship from the people who have given me the gift of theirs. I truly appreciate the friends that have gone out of their way to treat me as a normal person, and take the time to do normal things.

My childhood friends have hung in there with me. Chris Riordan, Steve Ulik, Dick Stadler, Loni and Chris Hagerup and so many great people from my hometown have been my cheerleaders and advocates. Hundreds of people from Whitefish Bay came together and held a fundraiser for me during my early recovery. My friends organized the gathering at Cahill Park. People I didn't even know, or remember, came to show their support. Each class reunion I've attended, I've been able to stand a little taller and walk a little further.

Through e-mail and social media, I've stayed in touch with long-time friends and gotten to know many others much better than before. It's amazing how a kind word or a holiday wish can make me feel so happy.

When he still lived here, my former neighbor Kendrick would come by and take me out to lunch. I would walk in and out of the restaurant with him. He didn't have to help me at all. Once there was a big curb to walk up and walk down. I was using the cane and I was taking forever. But he is a patient kind of guy. He'll help you forever no matter what is going on. He would go in front of me to get doors, and behind him by myself, I'd be wondering if I started to fall how the heck would he get me?! He always managed.

Kendrick also let me ride in the cart while he golfed, and even let me drive the cart. Once. Maybe I should not share that. But it was a lot of fun. We survived, but I am not a very good driver.

He even let me stay at his house when Susan was gone, and my daughters were at college. When we got to his house he let me walk into and around his house with my arm around him. This was back when I couldn't even use a cane. I stayed in the basement. He took me down to sleep and helped me upstairs in the morning.

We went camping with his son Rick, and I had a great time. He took me deep-sea fishing. He used to live a block away from where we currently live, but since he moved back to Texas, we do less together now. I can't imagine why he spent so much of his time helping me walk. He has always believed that I could do it and that I will continue to improve.

Patience

Roger Wilson has also taught me about friendship, but his greatest lesson has been the art of patience. I have worked with Roger a long time, since returning to Colorado. He may be the best listener I've ever known. Roger is truly the best help I've had standing and walking again. He is so helpful to me, and has stayed with me through all my ups and downs. He does all this for a small amount of money. I can't go on because the positive talk about Roger would take pages and pages. He might get embarrassed.

Patience is also a quality of my entire family, especially my older brother, Dave. He lives in Milwaukee. I don't see him once a week like I see Roger, but I wish I did. My family has been patient with me, and that has taught me to be more patient with them and others. Each person in my life has had their own experience of my TBI, and I have to remember how hard it has been for them. Everyone deals with it in their own way, and it took me a long time to see things from their perspective.

Coaching

I have known the best coaches in the world. My father Jack Hirst, my neighbor Greg Capper, my high school coach Jack Bleier, and Gregg Popovich, who went from the AFA to the NBA. These men demonstrated to me, through their words and deeds, what it means to be a coach.

Coaching isn't just about winning or losing. It's about discipline, boundaries, fundamentals and practice. Good coaches lead the way by setting good examples. The best coaches work just as hard as the team and care about each player as an individual contributing to the greater effort.

Coaching is not just about sports. Life requires good coaching. My wife may be the best personal coach in my life. She encourages me to push myself beyond the limitations TBI has presented, and others expected. And she believes in season tickets.

Generosity

I can honestly say if I had seen or heard someone asking for help before my accident, I would have given it. But anything I would or could have done pales in comparison to the amazing generosity shown to me and my family over the years.

The Air Force community, from the Academy days and through our careers, has been there always, most of the time anonymously and with no expectation of thanks or repayment.

Bob Sallis was and is a good friend since the basketball days at the Academy. He is now a doctor. Bob sent me a stretching mat and walking bars, which he bought from the money he collected from players and coaches from our team.

Acts of kindness and generosity such as this have been numerous, and it is humbling to learn what people will do for others from the kindness in their hearts.

Loyalty

My friends and family have all been loyal to me, and I am grateful. But the best teacher on loyalty was my beloved guide and companion, Nyla. I never had a pet as a child, and I had a lot to learn when she came into my life. She trained me.

No matter how many times I dropped something on the floor, she would pick it up. No matter how slow I was in getting her food or taking her out, she never seemed upset. She received a lot of attention from people wherever we went, but she knew I was her responsibility.

She was by my side when I wrote or watched TV, a loyal companion. I don't know if I could ever have another dog because she was so special.

Humor

Most people don't find a lot of humor in pain and suffering. TBI is no joke and I worry about all the other people who are experiencing traumatic brain injury and its realities. But some of the funniest things have happened to me while negotiating my way through life with it.

Like the guy that gave me money when I was at the ballgame. Or getting the end of my toe snipped off at the nail salon, though that did not seem funny at the time. Some of my falls have been monumental, and I guess I'm lucky I haven't injured myself even more. There is something so inevitable as you are falling, that it can be strangely comical. Like the time I missed the curb with my walker and took Roger down with me. Scary in some ways, but we still laugh about it.

The lesson is you have to keep going and keep trying. Get up after you fall. And try to find the humor, so others can too.

I left the Las Vegas story as one of the last background notes, because I think my friend Bobby Renaud is a genius at keeping the glass half full, literally and metaphorically. He keeps me laughing and I like to laugh. Maybe the joke is on traumatic brain injury, not the other way around.

OTHER PERSPECTIVES

Bobby Renaud, *Air Force Academy Friend and Pilot*

Not too long after Steve's visit to Louisville, he asked me if I still played cards. "I want to go to Vegas, Bobby!" I thought to myself if he could brave the crowds at Derby Days, once again, I was game. I called Susan to see if it would be all right to take him and she agreed.

About six weeks later, I flew out to get him. He and Susan met me at my arrival gate and we made our way over to the departure gate. We were excited for our next adventure. Susan gave us both a hug goodbye, as the gate agent rolled up a special narrow wheelchair designed to assist in boarding. No way.

Of course, he wants to walk down the aisle to his plane seat. Helping Steve walk was just a little bit awkward. I'm six feet, 195 pounds, but he's six-foot, three inches and around 240 pounds. Solid.

The only way I could control him was to get behind him and put him into a big bear hug. That way he could stand up and not put too much weight on his left side. We negotiated the aisle this way to 14C, where I plopped him gracefully into his seat.

I had booked a hotel in Vegas called "New York, New York!" I was not aware that one of its main features was a roller coaster. Steve took one look at it and his eyes just lit up. "Bobby, I want to go on the roller coaster!" I wasn't so sure that was the greatest idea, given the circumstances, but he was adamant. "No, really, Bobby—let's go!"

So I roll Steve up in his chair to the attendant and ask if it's all right to let Steve ride the roller coaster. The attendant looked at him, and shrugged. "Can he sit up?!" Steve and I said yes, and waited in a really long line, before we realized there was actually a line for handicapped access, with nobody waiting. This would come in handy later.

I haul Steve out of the chair, put him in the bear hug, move him to the roller coaster car, and strap him into the very front seat. Then I clamber in next to him, and off we went. His eyes got so big when we hit the first gut-twisting drop, just like a little kid. I was looking at him to make sure he didn't fly out, so I missed a lot of the immediate view, but watching him gave me the picture. He was screaming and drooling and laughing all at the same time, and when we hit the bottom, he's way down in the seat, sort of cork-screwed in by the G force. Not nine Gs like the Eagle, but enough to make it fun. I help him up and he beams at me. "Let's do it again, Bobby!"

I asked the attendant if we could just stay in the front seat to go again, but he said we had to get out and get back in, just like everyone else. So I had to run back, get the chair, throw Steve in, and get back in line. But this time we used the handicapped gate, cut in front of the longer line, and strapped ourselves right back in the front seat.

We repeated this routine about a dozen times. By then I was getting tired and a bit queasy, and thankfully, Steve was hungry.

We ate a nice meal, and then it was time to play cards. Back in our pilot training days, Steve was always a pretty decent poker player. That night, we hit the black jack table, and his inscrutable facial expressions, combined with his math ability, threw the crowd for a loop. Who was this guy in a wheelchair who ended up rolling away with about $600?!

By then, it was getting late. I had booked a handicapped accessible room and got Steve into the bed nearest to the bathroom. I melted into bed, ready to collapse. "Hey Bobby! Gotta go—need help!"

I wasn't exactly sure how much help he needed, but it was minimal. He needed help standing up, and I guided him back to bed, and off I went to my slumber. So I thought.

"Hey Bobby! I'm sore—Bobby, can you massage my shoulder?!" At that time, his left arm was still pretty curled up, and he couldn't straighten it out, not that over a dozen roller coaster rides could have helped. I've always had the magic fingers, so I dug in behind his left shoulder, and hit some muscle or nerve, and his left arm straightened completely out. Well, Steve was pretty impressed with that, so you guessed it, twenty-seven times later, he was perfectly happy and I was exhausted. I promised to take him to the spa in the morning so I could get some sleep.

The next day it was off to the spa. Steve was up for a massage, and I explained to the masseuse his condition, and described the sweet spot I had found that straightened out his arm. The guy said they didn't do physical therapy, and I looked at him and said "I bet you have in the past though, right?!"

So I left Steve for a half-hour massage, and found the sauna and the steam room. Over an hour later, Steve is rolled back in all happy and the smiling masseuse reports he "responded well." I think Steve must have tipped him a good percentage of his winnings from the previous night.

Then he sees the Jacuzzi. "Bobby! I want to get in. Help me get in!" Once again, I find myself asking an attendant if Steve can get in, but this time Steve and I don't have a stitch on. After waiving liability, I haul Steve out of the chair, put him in the bear hug and somehow get him into the Jacuzzi.

I had to prop him up in the corner and sit up next to him so he wouldn't tip over. We're sitting there enjoying the bubbles in our ten-foot-square tub. Eventually, another guy joins us in this fairly small body of water, looking at us warily. I felt obligated to go into my explanatory mode, describing our past as manly pilots, Steve's accident and somewhere along the line, I'm standing up to tell our story. When I pause to take a breath, I look over and Steve has disappeared. Well, without my support, he has slid under the water, his lips and nose are above the surface and he's sort of yelling my name. "Bobby—help!" Oops.

Another bear hug was required to haul Steve up out of the water and we make an ungainly naked exit from the tub. I plopped Steve back into his chair and we go to get dressed. As we wave adieu to our new friend in the tub, he says, I hope with admiration, "You fighter pilots really take care of each other!" I retorted, "Yeah, never leave your buddies behind!"

I guess I hadn't really thought about it much, but the guy was right. Steve was still my buddy, the same guy was still there no matter what the TBI had done to him, and we were still having one laugh after another. Maybe finding the humor in tragic situations is some sort of mechanism we flip on, because it is so important to keep looking for the good things.

Steve did tell me a sad story about a local retail clerk stealing money from him. He would need help getting money from his wallet when buying things, and the guy would turn his back and slip out extra money, thinking Steve wouldn't notice. Steve reported the guy, but sometimes I think people are so ready not to believe someone who appears to be damaged. On the other hand, there have been so many amazing people in his life who just take him as he is. There are many things he lost, but probably more things that nobody can take away from my buddy Blaster.

Susan Hirst, *Wife*

I never could have imagined what happened to our life when Steve came home, and I don't wish it on anyone. Steve and I had so many plans and dreams. Nothing fancy, just a relatively early retirement, then, a peaceful and comfortable life. We both thought we'd finish our Air Force careers and then move into either a small business (Steve wanted a beer and brats bar), or teaching and coaching professions. With our military retirements, we figured we wouldn't need much in the way of income, just enough to allow us to travel and do the things we enjoyed.

Still, my life is blessed. Today, our plans and dreams are actually very different. Steve is medically retired and I have retired with my pension, and work as a civilian doing the exact same job here at Peterson AFB, Colorado. We might have a small business someday, but at this point, all I really want is to relax when the time comes and we can do so. We have our home here in Colorado and we still have a house in Phoenix where we can eventually spend the winters.

This is not what I was prepared for but I'm handling it and actually doing OK. Probably the most difficult thing was that, early on, I didn't do enough things for myself. Specifically, exercise has always been very important to me, but with new schedules and responsibilities, that became inconsistent at best. I gained weight and lost fitness, because I didn't take the time I needed to get back and stay in shape. Being more realistic, maybe I'm not out of shape, just not in the shape I used to be. I've gotten better at balance and taking care of myself.

Another thing that has always made life so difficult is seeing all around us people living the lives we used to be living. We see families carelessly wander through malls and parks, dining out, or watching sporting events, and it has a huge impact on us. We do very little with that carefree air. Our issues are more stressful. When they were younger, our daughters resented Steve's injuries and how it took part of their dad away from them. Now, I realize the positive ways Steve's TBI has influenced their lives. We could not be prouder of how they have matured and the paths they have chosen.

Both Stephanie and Stacey are grown and out of the house. Steve likes being independent, has his routines, and doesn't need so many people doing things for him. So I work, while Steve stays home, sort of. He has plenty to do. He goes to the YMCA, the bank, the grocery store, Target, and the Veterans Affairs office all on his own, sometimes experiencing new adventures along the way.

Who knows what we'll do, but Steve did get a new special bike, a three-wheel trike, that he'll ride with the family on streets and trails. That may become our sport of choice. We both like to travel and with careful planning can find places that accommodate disabled, but it takes a lot of extra work.

We love attending sporting events together, visiting our daughters and family, and dearly love reuniting with our Air Force friends from all over the world. Writing this book has been good for Steve. Perhaps we can take what we've gained in life's experiences and help others to have fuller lives.

Steve and I are blessed. Our family has weathered our own private hell and I think we're likely better for it. Would I change the past and forgo the lessons we've learned and the friends we've made?! Absolutely! I couldn't do this if I knew what I was getting into, fortunately we can't change the past and we get to keep the friends. There are things I wouldn't change that surely resulted because of our experiences. Stacey is compassionate, interested in her dad and she pushes me to be better. She's a tough cookie. Stephanie is a softy and makes sure I'm taken care of. She worries about me, is concerned about my mind and my heart and lets me know that I matter. She pushes Steve to be better. We won!

Stephanie Mitchell, *Daughter*

Growing up in the Hirst family was amazing in so many ways. Looking back to my childhood, it is impossible to distinguish those things I thought and felt before the accident from the things I have known since. There is not a huge tragic line in my past where on one side all things are wonderful and the other horrific and miserable. I just have the memories of my childhood with no real delineation of when they were suddenly and drastically altered. I have plenty of memories, which are characterized by a not so "normal" family. My dad likes to talk about how perfect his life was before his accident, but nobody's life is perfect and hearing my dad talk about how great his once was is frustrating. I do not think his life was perfect and I have memories to back that up. I was far from the perfect daughter and that didn't start with the TBI. I also know I had a lot of great things in my life after my dad's accident that some of my classmates or peers did not, and I had them despite the fact that my dad had a TBI.

I can still clearly remember being in our kitchen in Alabama, a house I've driven by many times since, and getting the call you only imagine happens in the movies. From that night and throughout our time in Alaska, and even once we got to Minnesota, I do not think anyone realized the life that lay ahead. I have read other stories of brain injury victims. The notes or quotes from their families always make me ache. They are always so hopeful and positive. Their focus is on the broken bones or the coma, what they never talk about, what they couldn't possibly know, is that the coma just might be the easiest time. They are convinced that things will eventually return to the way they were before.

The truth is that no one ever stays the same, but in the case of a brain injury the changes are so rapid and irreversible. Those around a TBI victim do not have time to adjust to the changes, and probably for good reason. No one would stick around if they could see what was coming and tried to prepare. I truly believe that people grow into different versions of themselves over the course of a lifetime. My dad got in a car accident and was not given a lifetime to change, but it took at least a year to truly recognize that this change was more than a temporary symptom of the injuries he suffered in the accident. I actually can't remember a time when I thought he would get any "better."

We had plenty of support immediately after my dad's accident. It was that hopeful time when people showed up expecting their friend or brother to just wake up and hang out. I don't think reality settled in for a while but the visits definitely tapered off. Life is hard enough without the extra worry of a disabled and brain injured person to deal with and if you don't have to deal with it why subject yourself to it? At least that's the way I saw why people weren't present in my dad's life. Despite their extremely limited knowledge, everyone always knew just what we should be doing and how. Friends and family wanted to be able to control the situation, of course we all did, but it wasn't possible. They loved us and they only wanted what was best, but they could not have known what was best. While we were not a model family, it was still our family.

Now that I'm older than my parents were when they got married and had Stacey and I, it is hard for me to imagine them at the same point in their lives that I am, then having it all ripped away from them. I try hard not to think about it, it just isn't fair. I feel guilty sometimes, but more than that I hope and pray that my strength is never tested to that degree.

I know my parents wanted me to grow up, go to college, and be a successful functioning adult but I sometimes feel as though I've abandoned them. Things are easier for me now, but I'm so far away, I know things are not any easier, especially for my mom. The things I once had to deal with because I lived with him are no longer my hassle or burden.

Growing up with my dad was not even like growing up with an extra sibling. When I was young and selfish, I imagined it would all be better if he would just go away. I just wanted him to leave. As I got older I didn't care about any of it for myself, I just didn't understand what more could be done and where life could go for my mom. I still do not understand where their lives are supposed to go from here, but I truly do want them both to be happy.

Stacey Hirst, *Daughter*

My life is not my parents' life, not my family's life. For that, I have my parents to thank. I have my own life, one that is separate from, yet intertwined with theirs. My mom made a choice to stay and walk beside my dad throughout his life. But she never asked me to make that same choice. She let me leave when it was time and she lets me come back.

I often feel a sense of guilt for not being closer and more available to them. I know I am where I need to be to maintain a sense of self. My dad tells me often that he misses me. Sometimes he will call me multiple times in a day to say the same thing. In fact, I can recite the words he leaves on every message, "Hi Stace. It's your dad. Just calling to say hi. You don't have to call me back. Love you." Those are simple words. When I listen to them, I hear something much more profound. I hear, "Hi Stace. It's your dad. I'm calling because I'm here and you're not. And I miss you. I want to talk and I want to know what you've been doing today. You make me proud. Your life makes me proud. I wish you were here, but I'm glad you're there. And I want to share in it with you. You don't have to call me back, but I sure hope you do. I love you more than you could ever know." I have always known that both of my parents love me unconditionally. It is because of that love and all its intricacies that I am able to be the person I am and know that I will always be welcomed back and embraced by my parents regardless of where I am or what I am doing.

Everyone I've ever met has some tragedy to share. It may be seemingly simple, something others would scoff at and not accept as tragedy, but we've all experienced some sort of suffering. Whether that suffering is great or small, we go on living, we must. Our lives are always different than they once were, and always different than we planned. My dad has come a long way in sixteen years. He's written his story. I believe this is the best therapy he has received, far superior to any physical, speech, or occupational therapy. The best gift he could have possibly have given himself is here in these pages. He is not one to talk about his feelings. Maybe he never was. But his feelings are so rich, so beautiful, so painful, so encouraging. He has a voice that is not consumed by his physical limitations and it is so much more powerful.

I cannot really remember him that well before the accident. I have memories and I've heard stories and seen pictures, but the man I know to be my father is the man who has been my father for the majority of my life. I am twenty-five. For sixteen years of my life I have had a father with a TBI. A man who struggles to eat, walk, and speak. A man who spends his days in front of the computer typing things he is unable to say out loud. A man who travels the neighborhood in a power wheelchair smiling as he visits various neighbors. A man who goes to the YMCA and shows up everyone there by simply going through the front doors. I know that I loved the man he was before, because I can remember the excitement and comfort I felt whenever he was near. Our relationship has changed, as it was bound to do regardless of the circumstances. The man I have come to love as my father is the one on the cover of this book. And I love him more and more each day. The love I have for him is not because I am tied to who he once was, but because of who he is now.

My greatest desire for my father would be that he could see that he has an incredibly charmed life. He has suffered a lot, but he has also been given a lot and earned a lot. His passion to live is incredible. Not many people could maintain and recreate such a rich life after suffering such an incredible tragedy. That in itself is reason to celebrate. There is a reason that people have stayed close to him and a reason that he continues to draw more people into his life. He has so much that others desire and so much that attracts people to him. I could care less if the man never takes another step again. He doesn't need to walk. In comparison to what he's accomplished and the gifts he already has, walking is nothing.

Me and John Graaff, August 2011. *Photo by John Graaff.*

STILL STANDING— WHAT'S NEXT?!

I really am still standing. Sure, I need a power chair for the long hauls around the neighborhood and to the YMCA, and I am in a manual chair for events and travel. But I try to stand and walk as much as I possibly can. I know I scare some people with my efforts, because they think I'm going to wipe out and hurt myself more. And I know I annoy others, because it just takes me longer to do anything.

But my legs are much stronger and coordinated than they have been since my accident. Susan says my body is the strongest it has been since then, so the exercising I'm constantly doing to get my strength back is definitely paying off. I try like heck to be physically the same as I was, but it won't happen.

This injury took out of my brain many memories, which would have made me joyous when I thought of them. My friends tell me that just getting older means none of us are the same as we used to be. They assure me their memories play tricks on them too. Pretty soon we can all blame our memory loss on senior moments.

My speech is getting better all the time. People tell me they can now understand my speech, and I can tell when they can and cannot understand me.

I know how important walking is. So, I will keep trying to go further. I believe in my own heart a miracle was performed on me. Because, if anyone had seen me even eight years after my car accident, they would have wondered how I survived. A few doctors I've had just came right out and said "no 'fricking' way will you ever walk!" Never did appreciate those votes of confidence.

It has taken a lot of work just existing as I am. Folks notice how much better I'm doing physically and speech-wise, and that really makes me happy! I'm a believer in drawing inspiration from achieving goals. Goals push me to work hard, and not think so much about what might have been. Sometimes I don't accept my life as well as I should, but that is never a good place to be.

I know I have come a long way, but my goal is to keep IMPROVING. Just because I'm doing things nobody would have predicted, does not mean I will ever quit trying to do more. I would like to keep getting better physically and speech-wise in every way possible. Not to negate how far I've come, I'm still not comfortable with where I am. It was a long recovery from the knee replacement, but with Roger's supervision, I'm walking unaided around the three-point court at the YMCA, and sometimes for twenty to thirty yards with no assistance.

I recognize and appreciate the real blessings in my life. On the other hand, some regrets never fade and there are constantly new challenges. If I never had the accident I might still be in the Air Force. Or Susan might still be in, or getting out before she was able to retire. We might have both retired and started a bratwurst stand downtown, Blaster Brats or something.

Not flying really burns me up. We were such a group. Pilots hung around together, partied together, played sports together, and told personal secrets to each other. I miss the friendship and closeness terribly. Some guys are glad for it to be in their past—not me. Things then were very easy for me: flying, playing sports, coaching, even describing how I felt, were very easy for me. Now, everything is impossibly hard, harder than anything. I still am very angry, I think mostly at myself anyhow, for what has occurred to my physical well-being. I get really angry at no one special for what happened.

Being grounded from flying, from basketball, from all the blessings I took for granted, is something I will never totally accept. My Air Force friends and I have had some really wonderful times. They have helped me remember some of the amazing times we had by sending me these stories.

I thought I was waiting for a shoulder operation that I hoped would turn my life around. For years I have had excruciating neck pain and body pain, especially every time I work out. And I had a nagging shoulder injury before I was hurt that has only worsened in the last sixteen years. The pain has been unbearable at times, especially in my neck. But medical people either ignored me, didn't want me to get addicted to pain meds, or assumed it was just something I'd have to live with.

Just recently, while trying to alleviate my pain and locate a better place for injections, one of my doctors at the VA in Denver ordered an MRI. I was shocked to be told that the MRI revealed a large tumor on my brain, probably benign and slow-growing, but that will be the next hurdle in the recovery marathon. As I write these words, I am preparing for surgery to remove this tumor. So, stay tuned. I do realize my life is not over. And I have a lot left to enjoy. I love seeing both of my daughters doing things in life they truly enjoy. Our daughters are the best. Stephanie is married now to Pat Mitchell, a really great guy, and they are now part of the lifetime Air Force way. I am very proud of the fact that my wife Susan and my daughter Stephanie are the very first mother/daughter graduates of the Academy!

Our daughter Stacey is making a huge difference for the developmentally disabled adults and live-in assistants of the home where she lives and works. I am amazed by her abilities and very proud of her.

My beautiful wife and I find many things to do and enjoy together, like sports events, eating out and going to weddings and parties, and traveling. We have season tickets to the Air Force Academy football and basketball games, and we travel to see those games and to watch the San Antonio Spurs play so we can see Coach Pop.

We travel to reunions to see our families and childhood friends, and our Air Force family, especially my pilot buddies, and the friends and colleagues we made along the way that have truly become like family. The Air Force Academy is part of who we are and we are still so proud to be a part of it.

Flying in my mind. August 2011. *Photo by John Graaff.*

In August of 2011, I got a chance to go flying with a friend here in Colorado, John Graaff. At first when John invited me to fly with him in his airplane, and he said I could take the controls, I seriously wondered what was wrong with this guy. He knew I had been in a car crash and I had injured my brain. FLYING IS TOUGH ENOUGH WITHOUT A BRAIN INJURY! But I got a lot out of it thanks to John and his confident and trusting attitude. He is highly safety conscious and very knowledgeable about flying.

Overall, it was very enjoyable. I wasn't able to get my right hand to work correctly and it was such a small airplane that it reacted to every stick and rudder input and it took me a few seconds to adjust. In case you are wondering, the airplane had an airplane parachute, which could be deployed if something seriously went wrong with the airplane, or me.

Susan was there when we landed. John took some great photos. After flying we went to lunch at the Peterson AFB O' Club. John didn't want me to pay. But I insisted and paid for some of the flight cost and lunch. So overall, everybody had a fantastic time!

That was one great day of many in my life post car-crash. John says we'll go flying again sometime. I'd like that.

In many ways, every day is a new take-off. My life has been a beautiful, sometimes stormy, flight, with unexpected detours and destinations. My plan is to continue defying the odds, and to finally slip those surly bonds of earth as an old man, still surrounded by the ones I love.

If you as a reader made it this far, then you probably know someone with TBI. Maybe you have TBI. If not, you will certainly meet someone with TBI, and if you have not, reach out and find someone. Their story is in their head along with the injury. Take the time to listen. Look past the chair or the muscle spasms or the external signs that scare you or confuse you. There is a person in there just like me.

You see, I'm not just still standing. In my mind I am still flying. I have caressed the perfect faces of my daughters, I have loved looking into my wife's amazing green eyes, and I think I actually have touched the face of God.

[Editor's Note: While finishing his book, Blaster was diagnosed with a benign brain tumor. He underwent successful surgery on July 5, 2012 at the University of Colorado Health Sciences Center. He continues his recovery in Colorado Springs, where he is still standing, walking longer and longer distances, and speaking more clearly. To follow his progress, visit **Fans of Still Standing** on Facebook.]

ACKNOWLEDGMENTS

This book took a big team and a lot of coaching to get from my brain to the page. I would like to thank my starting line-up, especially my wife Susan and our daughters Stephanie and Stacey. If you have not figured out how much they mean to me, please go back and read the book again.

My mother Mag has been a direct line to the higher powers that continue to impact my life in blessed and mysterious ways. I am so very thankful to her and my late father Jack for a most positive upbringing and happy childhood.

I have a wonderful family, original and extended. I thank my brother Dave and my sister Sue for being such important early role models. I still look up to you both. My younger brothers Mike, Tom, and Dan have long been my best companions and competitors. I love you and all your families very much.

When I married Susan, I gained an incredible collection of new family members. I thank them all for everything they have done for me. My other mother, Lucille Roth and her late husband, Dave, have been parents to me in every way. I miss Dave very much and treasure Lucille's constant love and support.

Susan's brothers, Davey and Jeff, and sisters, Mary and Julie, and their families have been my own. Living in Colorado the past sixteen years gave me lots of opportunities to experience their generosity and love.

My first coach was my dad. There are several others who made a real difference in my life, teaching me the best ways to use my talents and appreciate the talents of others. To me, Greg Capper, Jack Bleier and Gregg Popovich, represent the ideals in coaching. Thanks to Greg for making me the youngest commissioner of basketball in any league, and to Jack for sticking to the fundamentals in basketball and in friendship. Coach Popovich, you are the class act of the NBA. Thanks to all of you for contributing to the book. I'd be happy to provide background notes or a foreword when you all write your books.

My first friends, including Chris Riordan, Steve Ulik, Dick Stadler, and Loni and Chris Hagerup, have remained some of my most loyal and treasured friends. To them and the many other friends and supporters from Whitefish Bay, I am humbled by your generosity and encouragement. Thanks for letting me lean on you in every way, some more heavily than others. Sorry for any inadvertent back injuries.

My military family is all over the world and they have been there in the good times and the hard times. My fellow fighter pilots are a true band of brothers. Their families are extensions of our own, and all continue to provide us with good times and treasured friendships.

To Howie Chandler, who witnessed the creation of my tac call sign—and I've been Blaster ever since. Pretty cool to know the former Vice Chief of Staff of the Air Force— thanks for sharing the original story of how "Blaster" came to be.

To Gabby and Ava Hayes, you surely outdid yourselves. Gabby, sometimes known as David, was my F-15 Squadron Commander at Kadena AFB in Okinawa. He and Ava have become even closer friends in recent years. Thanks for being two of my earliest readers and for your significant contributions to my book.

To Bob "Doc MacGuyver" Ireland, for your insight and service to the many military survivors of TBI, PTSD and their families, thank you. Keep speaking up.

To Bobby Renaud, thanks for your passion about my book and for helping my editor, Anni Ry, speak "fighter pilot." Tom Hogan, Jeff "Mange" Wilkerson, Tim Harris, Kmart Kresge, José and Karen Sims, and all the Air Force family who have helped me get this story out, I couldn't have done it without you.

The United States Air Force Academy is the cornerstone of my life in many ways. I value the education I received and am proud to be related to the first mother and daughter graduates of the USAFA, Lt Col Susan (Roth) Hirst, Ret., Class of 1983, and Captain Stephanie Mitchell, Class of 2007. We are proud to be alumni, and I am grateful for their help in completing my story, and my life.

My daughter Stacey makes me very proud every day. She has taken her own journey and given to others in ways most cannot begin to comprehend. Her contributions to my book and life are without measure.

The new friends I have met during my recovery have changed and improved my life in so many ways. Roger Wilson, my personal trainer and wingman, has kept me moving forward. Gene Arkfeld and Kendrick Sneckner have taken time to care for, entertain and motivate me. Thanks!

Colorado Springs has been a great home. Thanks to Springs Metro, my friends at the YMCA, Target, Safeway, Wells Fargo Bank, and the Air Academy Federal Credit Union. Many of my experiences have come while spending time with you. Our neighbors have picked me up, literally, more times than I can or want to count. You are great! I want to live in this neighborhood forever.

To the health care professionals who have saved my life, repaired me in endless ways, replaced spare parts and removed unwanted ones, and generally put up with me these many years, thank you for your dedication. Even those of you who thought I might never walk—you provided more inspiration than you know. I'm still working to prove you wrong!

In memory of Val Gardner, my speech therapist at HealthSouth. You were the best and the catalyst for me writing this book and bringing my service dog Nyla into my life.

The Veterans Administration represents mixed blessings through no fault of their own. Our country needs to provide far more support to the many veterans and their loved ones who rely on their care after service to our great nation.

To Anni Ry, I couldn't have done this without you. Your influence, assistance, and dedication are on every page. Thank you so very much! For anyone I left out, I'm sorry. You are always in my heart, if not in my memory.

ABOUT THE AUTHOR AND EDITOR

Major Steven R. Hirst (Ret.) grew up in Whitefish Bay, Wisconsin, and graduated from the United States Air Force Academy, where he was a member of the Falcons basketball team. His Air Force career included teaching, coaching and flying the F-15 Eagle. He lives in Colorado Springs, Colorado with his wife, Susan Hirst LtCol, USAF, Ret. He has two daughters, Stephanie Mitchell and Stacey Hirst.

Ann Ryan Solomon also grew up in Whitefish Bay, Wisconsin, and holds a BFA from Stephens College and an MA from the University of Missouri. An award-winning writer and editor, she lives in Creve Coeur, Missouri, with her husband Rick Solomon. Like Blaster, she has two lovely and talented daughters, Eileen Siobhan McClary and Gwyneth Muriel McClary.

Stay in touch through **Fans of _Still Standing_** on Facebook.

CPSIA information can be obtained at www.ICGtesting.com
Printed in the USA
BVOW081102170912

300628BV00002B/3/P